The Multinational Corporation and Social Policy

edited by
Richard A. Jackson
introduction by
Charles W. Powers

Published in cooperation with the
Council on Religion and International Affairs

The Praeger Special Studies program—
utilizing the most modern and efficient book
production techniques and a selective
worldwide distribution network—makes
available to the academic, government, and
business communities significant, timely
research in U.S. and international economic, social, and political development.

The Multinational Corporation and Social Policy

Special Reference to General Motors in South Africa

PRAEGER SPECIAL STUDIES IN INTERNATIONAL ECONOMICS AND DEVELOPMENT

Praeger Publishers   New York   Washington   London

Library of Congress Cataloging in Publication Data

Council on Religion and International Affairs Consulta-
    tion on Corporation Responsibility, Airlie House, 1972.
    The multinational corporation and social policy:
special reference to General Motors in South Africa.

    (Praeger special studies in international economics
and development)
    Includes bibliographical references.
    1. General Motors Corporation.   2. Corporations,
American—Africa, South.   3. Industry—Social aspects—
Case studies.   I. Jackson, Richard A., ed.   II. Title.
HD9710.U54G385   1972   658.4'08   73-18872

PRAEGER PUBLISHERS
111 Fourth Avenue, New York, N.Y. 10003, U.S.A.
5, Cromwell Place, London SW7 2JL, England

Published in the United States of America in 1974
by Praeger Publishers, Inc.

The Council on Religion and International Affairs (CRIA) was founded in 1914 by Andrew Carnegie in an effort to bring religious principles to bear on the problems of world peace. Through a basic program of conferences and publications CRIA has through the years played a small but vital role in attempting to bring moral precepts to international affairs as envisaged by its founder.

Several years ago, together with many other philanthropic and nonprofit institutions, CRIA began to study its portfolio, which contains securities of international corporations, from a moral perspective. Discussions attending its social investment concerns resulted in the conviction that CRIA should and could further the important and difficult discussion on the ethics of investment by organizing a seminar. Out of this first seminar came the book People/Profits: The Ethics of Investment. The current volume is the result of a second such seminar. These two seminars in turn have helped CRIA to embark on a full-scale Corporate Consultation Program, which concerns itself with the social responsibility of multinational corporations.

This book is one result of the second in a series of consultations on corporate responsibility and the multinational corporation being conducted by the Council on Religion and International Affairs (CRIA). Out of the first consultation in this series came the book edited by Dr. Charles W. Powers and published by CRIA, People/Profits: The Ethics of Investment.

It is our conviction that whenever the multinational corporation and societal interests intersect, as they do increasingly, an ethical issue almost always emerges which needs concerted study. As a contribution to this immense and demanding task CRIA brings together--in discussions which produce both heat and light--corporate executives, leaders of organized labor, representatives of government, religious leaders, and social ethicists. We hope that this book, which developed from one such discussion, together with People/Profits and other projected CRIA publications, will contribute to the small but growing body of literature dealing with ethical issues related to the world of corporations.

This book contains both prepared papers and abridged discussion from a three-day consultation sponsored by CRIA at Airlie House, Airlee, Virginia. Consultation participants, whose names and organizational affiliations are listed on pages ix-x, attended in their individual capacities and not as representatives of the diverse public and private institutions that employ them or of which they are members. They do, however, represent a wide cross-section of opinion on the issues discussed: the social responsibilities of corporations and of their shareholders. The participants are active at the policy level of corporations, organized labor, government, and several types of nonprofit institutions: churches, universities, foundations. Each participant was chosen because of his recognized capability of contributing to the discussion. Each had an opportunity to read the manuscript of this book before agreeing to have his name included.

A number of persons contributed to the success of the consultation and to the preparation of the book. We wish to express, in the name of the CRIA Board of Trustees, our warm thanks to them.

To Dr. Powers, Associate Professor of Social Ethics at Yale Divinity School and CRIA's consultant on the general subject of corporate responsibility and the multinational corporation, who wrote the Introduction. Dr. Powers is also a member of the Committee on Financial Investments, United Church of Christ. He is the author of <u>Social Responsibility and Investments</u> and, with John G. Simon and Jon P. Gunnemann, of <u>The Ethical Investor: Universities and Corporate Responsibility</u>, as well as editor of <u>People/Profits: The Ethics of Investment</u>, a book published by CRIA on the first consultation it held on this topic.

To E. M. Estes, executive vice president of General Motors, and Byron E. Grant, then General Manager of Braden Copper Company, Kennecott Copper Corporation, for their lucid presentations of case studies. (We regret that space strictures made it impossible to include "Kennecott in Chile" in this book.)

To Terrance Hanold, Raymond Bauer, and Roger F. Murray, who wrote papers, distributed in advance of the consultation, which formed the base for discussions.

To Richard Jackson, the editor of this book, whose skillful craftsmanship developed a readable and useful study out of hundreds of pages of stenotypic transcript.

To the rapporteurs, Jon P. Gunnemann and L. Lincoln Eldredge, who so perceptively helped to guide discussion into rewarding exchanges.

To W. Howard Chase, who as chairman of the committee on the social audit led its members into dialogue which, when summarized for the entire group, advanced the discussion.

To Florence Norton, copy editor of <u>Worldview</u>--who made valuable contributions to the quality of the book.

If, as seems clear, the multinational corporation is one of the most powerful organizational forms in today's world, its potential impact on international society, quite apart from its profit-making capacity, is self-evident. It is our expectation that CRIA's three-year project on the multinational corporation and corporate responsibility--together with this book and its forerunner, <u>People/Profits</u>--will help to develop the international norms needed when dealing with the complexities of the multinational corporation.

PARTICIPANTS IN THE CONSULTATION

Held in Airlie, Virginia, 15-17 October 1972

Raymond Bauer
Harvard Business School

W. Howard Chase
Vice President
American Can Company

Anthony W. Connole
Administrative Assistant to
  Vice President Douglas
  Fraser
United Auto Workers

J. Howard Craven
Senior Vice President
Federal Reserve Bank
(now Senior Vice President
  and Economist, Union Bank)

Herbert H. Dow
Secretary
Dow Chemical Company

L. Lincoln Eldredge
Department of Theological
  Ethics
Andover Newton Theological
  School

Elliott M. Estes
Executive Vice President
General Motors Corporation

Stephen B. Farber
Assistant to the President
Harvard University

Kenneth P. Finnerud
The Rockefeller Foundation

Horace E. Gale
Treasurer
Department of Finance
American Baptist Home
  Mission Societies

Byron E. Grant
General Manager
Braden Copper Company
(now Chairman, Peabody
  Coal Company)

Thomas A. Guith
General Motors Corporation

Jon P. Gunnemann
Department of Religious
  Studies
Pennsylvania State Uni-
  versity

Terrance Hanold
Chairman, Executive
  Committee
The Pillsbury Company

Kirk O. Hanson
President
National Affiliation of
  Concerned Business
  Students

Robert M. James
Director, Corporate Planning
Xerox Corporation

Charles M. Judd
President
Breneman, Inc.

James E. Lee
Executive Vice President
Gulf Oil Corporation
(now President)

W. Putnam Livingston
Bankers Trust Company (ret.)

Bevis Longstreth
Debevoise, Plimpton, Lyons
 & Gates

Philip A. Loomis
Securities and Exchange
 Commission

A. William Loos
President, CRIA

Charles L. Marburg
Chairman, CRIA Subcommittee
 on Investment Policy

Donald F. McHenry
Carnegie Endowment for
 International Peace

Philip W. Moore
Project on Corporate
 Responsibility
(now in private law practice)

Roger F. Murray
Graduate School of Business
Columbia University

Robert T. O'Connell
General Motors Corporation

Robert S. Potter, Esq.
Partner
Patterson, Belknap & Webb

Charles W. Powers
Department of Social Ethics
Yale Divinity School

Martin Prochnik
Special Assistant to the
 Secretary
Department of the Interior

Patricia Cayo Sexton
Sociology Department
New York University

Michael P. Sloan
Special Assistant to the
 President
CRIA

Richard B. Smith, Esq.
Davis, Polk & Wardwell

Timothy Smith
Staff Director
Interfaith Committee on
 Social Criteria and
 Investment
also representing the
 Corporate Information
 Center
 National Council of
 Churches

Robert G. Walker
former Economic Adviser
U.S. Embassy
Santiago, Chile

Robert W. Worcester
Vice President
Federal Reserve Bank

CONTENTS

INTRODUCTION
Charles W. Powers

A hurried reader of this book may be led by a quick
perusal of the table of contents to proceed immediately
to the discussion of General Motors in South Africa to be
found in the final section. There, one may surmise, is
the real heart of the 1972 CRIA Conference on Corporate
and Investor Responsibility. If you are this hurried
reader, you will not be disappointed, for in the scope of
thirty pages you will find a complete and polished description of a corporate effort to respond to a controversial
social issue and one of the frankest and most rewarding
exchanges between corporate managers and business critics
to be found in the literature.

You will meet in this discussion not only E. M.
Estes, Executive Vice President of General Motors, whose
operating responsibilities until the fall of 1972 included
the company's operations in South Africa, but also some of
the most knowledgeable and active observers and critics of
GM policy. Among them are Donald McHenry, whose work at
the Brookings Institution has focused primarily on U.S.
corporate presence in Southern Africa; Robert Potter, the
corporate lawyer who as a layman led one of the national
boards of the Episcopal Church into a 1972 proxy controversy with GM on its South African operations; Philip
Moore, a director of the Project on Corporate Responsibility, which has submitted proxy resolutions on social policy to GM stockholders since 1970; and Timothy Smith, a
leader of many national church efforts to change U.S. corporate policy in Southern Africa over almost a decade.
Rare is the context in which informed persons with importantly divergent assessments of a corporate social policy
engage in face-to-face discussion. And even rarer is the
publication of such an exchange. Where discussion of a
topic is dominated by confusions and generalities--and
corporate social responsibility is such a topic--a well-
argued debate on an actual case is a welcome relief.

But if in your hurry you should follow the impulse
to delete, you will be deprived of much of the contribution this book makes to our understanding of the modern
corporation. Case studies can bring to light factors ignored or misunderstood in ethereal theorizing; but they
can easily be turned into superficial evidence by

muckrakers or hucksters. Case studies need a conceptual context, and this book provides one.

In Part I Terrance Hanold, then President of the Pillsbury Company and now chairman of its executive committee, depicts in remarkably perceptive and candid terms the impact of the computer on the organization of corporate decision-making and on the role of executive management. This paper not only gives a sense of how at least one executive views the responsibilities of, and restraints upon, decision-making in this new context, but also gives a sense of how the corporate manager perceives the role and competence of the outside corporate critic.

Perhaps Hanold's most notable assertion is his insistence that the power of the top level of management is severely circumscribed. This in itself is hardly new. In the 1950s, John Kenneth Galbraith observed in <u>American Capitalism: The Concept of Countervailing Power</u> that "the privilege of controlling the actions or affecting the incomes and property of others is something that no one of us can profess to seek or admit to possessing." What Hanold adds to our understanding is evidence not only that this self-depiction is still alive and well, but also that the computer model, by dispersing and "rationalizing" decision-making, has created an organizational pattern that can be effectively employed to buttress this managerial contention.

As the discussion of the paper demonstrates, many of the nonmanagement conferees are not prepared to abandon the notion that executive management either can or does shape corporate policy much more fundamentally than Mr. Hanold avers. Hence we see these participants pressing for much greater self-consciousness on the part of management about their impact on corporate practice. One is reminded in this discussion of Brandeis's admonition that corporate managers conceive of themselves as professionals who use their discretionary power for the public interest. Mr. Hanold is, however, consistently supported in his interpretation by his managerial colleagues, and their remarks are reminiscent of the comment attributed to President Kennedy after he had been convinced of the desirability of a new administration policy: "Now, let's see if we can get the Administration to buy it."

Surely one of the great dilemmas of leaders of large bureaucratic institutions is the difficulty of getting top-level policy, especially innovative policy, implemented. When these innovations involve not merely alterations in procedure but alterations in both goals and measuring instruments as well the dilemmas are compounded. Yet in the pressure to introduce social considerations into areas of the fabric of corporate decision where they have never before been a determining factor, there are precisely such new goals and yardsticks. Whether or not Hanold has underestimated the degree to which corporate executives shape the "character" of a corporation, it is clear that new departures in social policy cannot depend on the managerial conscience alone. "People," however important, are not the single key to institutional responsibility. Some standards for charting and measuring corporate performance are required, as is the creation of decision-making processes or mechanisms to relate those standards to a specific corporate context and to monitor progress toward them.

Raymond Bauer's work on the corporate social audit enabled the conferees to probe the first of these two additional components. No commentator is more aware than this Harvard Business School professor that "social audit" is a term seeking both definition and specification. Under its banner have gone diverse efforts to quantify corporate social practices of many varieties and kinds. The reader of this book will doubtless want to pursue the examination of the concept along the many paths traced by Bauer and his co-author, Dan H. Fenn, Jr., in their forthcoming book, The Corporate Social Audit.

But in the pages devoted to this topic in Part II of this book, three aspects of the "Can we measure social performance?" question are stressed: (1) Given the plural value systems in which corporations generally, but multinational corporations particularly, now operate, is it even possible to develop a single set of principles or standards against which corporate practices might be measured? Those who found societal pluralism to be irreducible tended to concede that no meaningful audit was in the offing and opted instead for greater disclosure of information about corporate activities that diverse communities and constituencies could then subject to differing standards. Others remained hopeful that, on at least some levels and in respect to some policies, commonly accepted standards could be found. (2) What aspects of corporate activity should be included in an audit? In the first attempts to develop audits made either by corporations themselves or by outside groups, stress has been laid on evaluation of the effectiveness and extent of the easily identified and conspicuous social programs inaugurated by corporations in recent years. Some

conferees played down the importance of these studies and
urged that the social auditors devote themselves to learning how to measure the social costs or benefits of regular
corporate operations. (3) Still, the question that dominated the consultation dialogue on the social audit question was, "Who should conduct these measuring efforts and
to whom should the audit results be disclosed?" The
"inside-outside" theme that is generated in the Hanold
paper and discussion is, then, a key issue also when the
question of establishing standards and testing adherence
to them is raised.

This same theme reappears importantly in Part III,
where the focus is on how social considerations should be
structured into corporate organizational patterns. This
issue was generated for the conference by Roger Murray's
attempt to consider whether one part of one constituency
of the corporation, its large institutional stockholders,
should attempt to raise social policy questions. Murray,
a Columbia Business School professor and a highly re-
garded institutional investor and trustee, is driven by
his analysis to the conclusion that a new structure, advisory to both management and the stockholder, is required. The key to his proposal is the stipulation that
such an advisory panel would publish its recommendations.
His suggestion initiated a conference-long debate on
which of two structural approaches to introducing social
considerations into corporate processes was desirable and
most important. The first approach would focus more on
the development of the internal mechanisms needed to secure for management itself sufficient input and advice
concerning the social impact of the corporation. The
second approach avers that the primary need is for structural changes that bring the views, influences, and even
representation of external groups into corporate decisions
on social questions and that make available to nonmanagement groups information that management itself might not
be disposed to reveal.

Perhaps the majority of conferees favored some combination of these two approaches. But, as the discussion
shows, there was no consensus on how these two types of
structure should be related and which combination of the
mechanisms now being proposed in corporate responsibility
discussions should be adopted. General Motors served as
an impromptu case study on this issue, too; indeed, the
complex of issues involved is most specifically delineated
in the discussion of the functioning and efficacy of GM's
new Public Policy Committee.

Whether, then, the topic is people, principles, or process, all three of the more "theoretical" parts of this book combine to raise one important issue: How, on the one hand, can economic institutions in this society become more responsive to changing social concerns unless they simultaneously disclose more information about their practices and become more receptive to the influence of societal groups that stand outside of the management process? But how, on the other hand, can economic institutions function efficiently if their goals are not constant and clear-cut, and unless decision-making is streamlined to pursue those goals? Into this dilemma comes a new social dynamic that was only beginning to emerge in the fall of 1972; its "acronym" is Watergate. It is impossible to believe that so traumatic an event in the public sector will not ultimately shape society's very basic attitudes toward the functioning of institutions in other sectors of society as well.

It is likely that the recent interest in corporate responsibility and responsiveness will shift somewhat and the focus will be sharpened on the question of corporate accountability. If this is so, then the recurrent "disclosure" theme in the first three parts of this book will be the dominant issue in future discussions of business policy. We are seeing an early indication of this as the pressures mount for fuller public disclosure of the factors that have created the energy crisis in general and the gasoline shortage in particular. The discussions that our "hurried reader" will be tempted to bypass will become increasingly timely and important.

Accountability can be said to depend on four factors: (1) adequate information to allow informed input into decision-making; (2) adequate "points of entry" for that input; (3) feedback to those interested in the decisions reached and explanation of how various factors were weighted in reaching the decision; and (4) mechanisms to allow the ultimate recourse of installing new leadership if a reconciliation between those held to account and those to whom they are accountable cannot be reached. Effective corporate leadership in a context where accountability is a key concern will be leadership that so effectively develops the first three factors that attention need not be focused on the fourth one. It will be leadership that inspires public confidence in its ability to "hear" what is being said from many directions, that is able to integrate those inputs into economic decisions, and that is capable of articulating in clear and

understandable ways the rationale for its policy. But
such leadership will not in all likelihood be possible
unless new ways can be devised for articulating social
goals and measuring performance in relation to them and
unless mechanisms are developed for structuring in the
social concerns of a citizenry which is rapidly losing
confidence in the good faith of the institutions that are
supposed to serve it.

The foregoing is perhaps an overlong plea that for
those who would seek to understand the significance of
the GM South African discussion, and any others that lie
on the horizon, the practice must be understood in the
context of the people, the principles, and the process
that shape it. The relationship between what is good for
General Motors and what is good for the U.S.A., let alone
the rest of the world, must be evaluated with the help of
these broader understandings.

Richard Jackson has done excellent work in pulling
hundreds of pages of transcript and preconference papers
together into a coherent and readable primer on corporate
social policy. But, it should be stressed, he was aided
in this effort by the organizing concepts--people, principles, process, and practice--that were first used by
Jon Gunnemann to help sharpen the discussion at the consultation itself. One can gain some comprehension of
Professor Gunnemann's ability simultaneously to synthe-
size and to draw distinctions in his summary of the discussion of Part I. Obviously abridged papers and abridged
discussions leave the views of an author or a speaker be-
reft of the qualifications made possible by an unedited
transcript. Hence, although the statements of the participants reprinted here may faithfully represent their
individual views on a very specific topic, fairness requires that care be taken neither to see these abbrevi-
ated comments as suggestive of a participant's more general views nor to take them out of context.

PEOPLE: CORPORATE MANAGERS AND THEIR RESPONSIBILITIES

The demands made on executive management in the increasingly complex area of large corporation activity are
many-faceted. With the corporation occupying a central
and extremely significant position among the various institutions that order and service contemporary developed
and developing nations, numerous societal forces, representing divergent interests, look at the large business
enterprise as both the answer to current needs and the
cause of current ills. Terrance Hanold's abridged paper
seeks to ferret out and clarify a manager's own view of
the areas in which corporate management wields power and
bears responsibility. To understand these questions, the
paper argues, one must first discern the radical shifts
in decision-making procedures that computers have brought
about in corporate contexts. Though not all participants
in the seminar concurred with Mr. Hanold's outline, it
was generally accepted as a fair analysis of present management decision-making schemes.

The Hanold paper provided the background for a lively
discussion which had several foci, including the leadership role of the corporate executive, the numerous "publics" with which management must deal, the corporate
ethos and climate of decision-making, the difficulty of
arriving at ethical standards and norms by which to judge
or regulate corporate activities, and the question of who
is to bring ethical considerations into business thinking
and operations. The answers one gives to these questions
are often shaped by one's conception of how much power
managers wield, as the excerpts from the conference discussion that form most of Chapter 2 make clear.

Jon Gunnemann's summary of the discussion sets the
stage for the broader debate of many of the corporate responsibility issues that follows later in this book. In
drawing the distinction between corporate policy and
ethics, Professor Gunnemann poses the difficult question,
"Is there a fundamental incompatability between the interests of a business organization and ethical demands?"
This question remains at the heart of all debate on corporate social responsibility.

1

THE CORPORATE MANAGER: A BUSINESSMAN'S VIEW
Terrance Hanold

If I am to illuminate in any degree the subject I have been asked to discuss, we must first reach an understanding respecting one or two of the terms used to state the topic and to deal with the argument.

Our interest at this conference does not embrace every business enterprise or every manager. It is limited to those firms of a size and duration sufficient to make some significant impact on the social dynamic of the general community. This less inclusive class of organization almost invariably uses the corporate form of identity.

A corporation, whether industrial, governmental, educational, religious, or nonprofit, is an imaginary entity existing only in the contemplation of law. While insubstantial, a corporation has a basis in reality because of the general understanding, formed out of experience, that numbers of people continuously engaged in the furtherance of shared objectives collectively constitute an entity separate from the personality of any of its members. A corporation is distinguished from the general run of associations because it satisfies specific conditions and obligations imposed by law, and has conferred on it certain qualities and powers defined by law.

The manner in which business corporations pursue their purposes and the degree to which they succeed in

Mr. Hanold is Chairman of the Executive Committee, The Pillsbury Company, in Minneapolis. He joined the company in 1946. He is on the Board of Directors of the Minneapolis Symphony and of the Institute of Ecumenical and Cultural Study.

them is a matter for public review. Since they exist only by reason of an act of the state, their purposes must serve the interests of the public, even though the objectives of the founders are primarily their own advantage. Whether a business corporation serves both the interest of the public and the advantage of its owning and operating communities is a question for which its management is primarily answerable.

While the field to which a particular corporation may address itself is of necessity left to the discretion of those who enter into the corporation, the public nonetheless has the right to insist that the fashion in which the affairs of the corporation are conducted is consistent with the values and objectives of the society it purports to serve. And those conducting its affairs must recognize those values and objectives in the plans they make and the courses of action they follow.

Thus a business corporation must be receptive and responsive in its relations to the public. Furthermore, it must be perceptive and responsible. This concept may be described as one of essential policy rather than as an ethic, but it is a policy that shapes fundamentally the ethic which governs action.

Where these questions of policy come for answer within a corporation has to do with its organization.

ORGANIZATION

To the outsider, corporate organization is a matter of grouping people by function and of arraying them within their function by steps according to their rank. From habit and history we tend to think of organization in bureaucratic terms, as a hierarchy in pyramidal form with successive levels of power and authority. This is, after all, the classic model on which the church, the state, and the military are built. There are still areas in a business corporation that operate, and quite properly, in a bureaucratic fashion. Those who control them I would describe as administrative managers. Their function is to preserve the routine and to maintain things as they are so far as the matters under their control are concerned. But the place for this kind of manager is diminishing, for the areas secure from change are few, and the computer is able to manage the routine with greater reliability, far greater speed, and much less friction than its administrative management counterpart.

Aside from taking over the repetitive performance of managerial acts, the computer has fundamentally altered the corporate structure by providing a far more effective communications system than the hierarchical structure afforded to the management side of the business. The two accompanying charts demonstrate my point.

The classic management design contemplated information flowing up the ladder, directions coming down, and performance reports going back. Only the people at the top had access to all the data out of which direction and control are fashioned; hence all decisions of consequence had to clear at the apex of the pyramid. Clearly the computer doesn't work that way. The information flows from its point of origin directly to the data base and directly out in processed form to whoever has need of it. Contrary to the vertical movements contemplated in the classical design, a tremendous amount of data and information moves laterally from source to action point today. Consequently it is becoming the rule that decisions are usually made short of the apex. Those involved in the origin of the issue and its solution communicate directly, regardless of organizational boundaries, and collaborate in the decision without consultation with their superiors. The constraints of time will not permit otherwise.

This means that the executive is less concerned with the particular decisions that the middle manager makes and more concerned with the extent and quality of the data base he uses, the analytical systems applied to the data, the decisional guides that affect his selection of alternatives, and the caliber of the associates and the character of the expertise that collaborate in making his decision.

Thus the computer has been a major force for change. Its advent has mechanized a host of routine tasks, and in the process has substantially diminished the administrative functions of the managers who supervised them. By shifting the center of emphasis from the supervision of people to the attainment of objectives it has caused managers to shift their areas of concern from procedural to professional matters--to the inquiry into the what and the why of things rather than the how.

So the crystallizing principle in corporate organizations is that decisions are participatively made by those involved according to the flow of information and the talents required, regardless of structure. Again this may be viewed as a principle of corporate policy rather than as an ethic, but it is a policy that nonetheless fundamentally shapes the ethic of management itself.

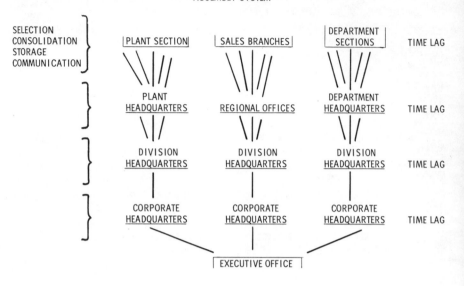

STANDARD INFORMATION
ASSEMBLY SYSTEM

SELECTION
CONSOLIDATION
STORAGE
COMMUNICATION

| PLANT SECTION | SALES BRANCHES | DEPARTMENT SECTIONS | TIME LAG |

PLANT HEADQUARTERS   REGIONAL OFFICES   DEPARTMENT HEADQUARTERS   TIME LAG

DIVISION HEADQUARTERS   DIVISION HEADQUARTERS   DIVISION HEADQUARTERS   TIME LAG

CORPORATE HEADQUARTERS   CORPORATE HEADQUARTERS   CORPORATE HEADQUARTERS   TIME LAG

| EXECUTIVE OFFICE |

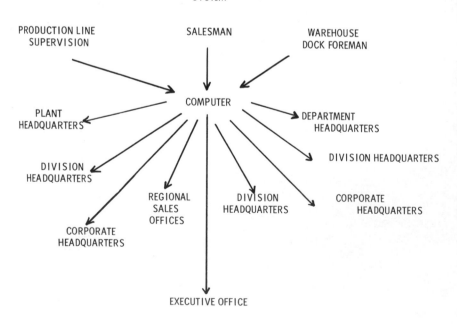

COMPUTER INFORMATION
SYSTEM

PRODUCTION LINE
SUPERVISION   SALESMAN   WAREHOUSE
DOCK FOREMAN

COMPUTER

PLANT
HEADQUARTERS   DEPARTMENT
HEADQUARTERS

DIVISION HEADQUARTERS

DIVISION
HEADQUARTERS

REGIONAL
SALES
OFFICES   DIVISION
HEADQUARTERS   CORPORATE
HEADQUARTERS

CORPORATE
HEADQUARTERS

EXECUTIVE OFFICE

6

MANAGEMENT

The active cultivation of the business of a corporation and the whole body of decisions and actions which
that entails fall, of necessity, to its management. While
the character of a corporate manager parallels that of the
entrepreneur in his functions of innovation and risk-taking,
there are vital differences between them: The entrepreneur
is expected to manage for his own profit, while the corporate manager is required to manage for the benefit of the
community of interests that comprise the corporation or
depend on it.

In describing the organization of corporate management we have noted the essential difference between the
hierarchical organization chart based on status and the
operative organization network based on informational relationships. While the trend toward professionalism en-
courages an equality in dignity among managers, differences in function permit a few broad classifications even
in a dynamic network.

While authority is widely dispersed in the business
firm that disqualifies status as a workable basis for
classification, there is a natural method of arraying managers proceeding from the character of his objectives and
the depth of the time horizon within which he works.
Thus, viewing managers in their action role rather than
in their organization boxes, we may divide them into five
groups.

1. At the supervisory level the manager oversees
the performance of repetitive operations by a subunit.
He has some discretion respecting the scheduling of the
work, the disposition of his staff, and the motivation
of the personnel. His objectives are set and his methods
are fixed, and he operates within a planning horizon not
exceeding a month. As I would put it, he manages by the
manual.

2. The middle manager has charge of a function and
directs the daily flow of transactions with other functions or operations of the firm and with the world outside. He participates in setting the goals established
for his function but cannot unilaterally change them.
His planning horizon is about one to six months. He has
considerable latitude in selecting the methods and resources for the attainment of those goals. He makes the
operating decisions for his department according to the
flow of information reporting events affecting his function.

He must respond quickly to constantly changing conditions. He manages by selective action.

3. The general manager has operational responsibility for a division or subsidiary. While he may participate to some degree in the conduct of daily affairs, he must essentially rely on middle management to carry on current business. He makes the benchmark decisions for his division, sets the objectives for middle management, allocates resources, delegates authority, monitors the ongoing performance of the business, appraises the forward options open to the division, and develops and recommends plans according to the guidelines determined by corporate policy. Within the limits imposed by corporate strategy and the resources at his disposal, the general manager has full authority to set the fundamental objectives for his business over its operational horizon-- about 18 to 36 months ahead--and has full accountability for the performance of his organization against those goals. He manages by objective.

4. The executive manager--top management--is responsible for the performance of all functions and operations of the firm (but has little direct oversight of them), and for the formation and execution of the strategy established for the survival and success of the corporation over the plannable future. Depending on the nature of the firm, his effective planning horizon may reach out five to twenty years. The executive manager ordinarily takes no more than incidental participation in the middle management area, and no more than intermittent participation in the general management area. His prime task is to measure the performance of the several lines of business comprising the firm, to evaluate the opportunities and hazards facing the firm, to assess the firm's future capabilities, to select the longer-term goals for the company, to plan the long-term action directions by which the corporation will attain them, and to arrange the resource acquisitions and personnel development which these objectives demand. Since opportunity must be sought outside as well as inside its present lines, and since the forecast of the future social, economic, and competitive environments is critical to the selection of the right opportunities, he must exercise insight as well as foresight. The executive practices management by perception.

5. The staff manager works within the time horizons and the resource limits and the objective frames of the several classes of managers with whom he is involved from time to time. He has a responsibility for the quality of

the decisions reached by the managers he advises, but he is not responsible for making or executing decisions. He manages by persuasion.

This tends to describe the areas of action and of single accountability at the several levels of management. But a description of their "turfs" by no means recognizes their areas of interaction and of shared responsibility. We recognize this in our firm by stating that a manager is not only specifically answerable for the attainment of the objectives assigned him, but is also generally re-sponsible for the attainment of objectives assigned other managers where he has the capability of a constructive addition to their efforts. And this duty is owed not only to his peers but to every other manager as well.

The increasing freedom with which this interaction occurs justifies the new habit of describing business or-ganizations as horizontal rather than pyramidal in design. This working parity in standing among managers furthers, of course, the trend to professionalism I have mentioned. And this professional character is a critical considera-tion in defining the ethical burden of management. For the professional assumes obligations that the workman does not.

It is of the essence of a profession that its prac-titioners have an expert knowledge in a field of public importance and that they recognize an obligation in the conduct of their practice not only to their clients or employers but to the public as well. The public impor-tance of corporate management is asserted rather than dis-puted by ally and antagonist alike. But there is little agreement, nor much principled disagreement, among friends or foes respecting our public obligations.

Since I have excluded the executive from the immedi-ate direction of most of the activities of his firm, what function is left to him and what is its ethical content? Clearly, the action decisions are centered outside the executive group, but in consequence these other manage-ment cadres are held to relatively short-term concerns. Hence the long-term decisions are reserved to the execu-tive group. These will control the action decisions of tomorrow just as the forward decisions made three to ten years ago control the action decisions made today.

Decisions directed to the immediate and the particu-lar must comply with long-term policies and standards, but they are not suited to the development of canons of conduct. So action decisions must consider whether they

conform to law and morals, but they are not suited to the
enunciation of ethical principles. Concepts of this kind
are necessary adjuncts to control decisions made for the
long term. Therefore the determination of the ethical
standards that will control specific corporate decisions
must be made by those charged with formulating control
decisions.

Clearly the area of ethical determination within the
corporation is the direct responsibility of its executive
management. It is an area of determination that they
must discharge in behalf of the corporation so that it may
discharge its duty to the public. It is an area of determination that they must discharge in their own behalf as
professionals directly obligated to the public to perform
their functions in a fashion advancing the public interest. They ought not, and do not, make these decisions
without the counsel of other managers who also have a professional interest in these matters, but the executive
managers must make these decisions and answer for them as
well.

In granting him a time horizon of five to twenty
years, I have obviously accorded to the executive the responsibility for forward planning beyond the immediate
reach of the present pursuits of the corporation. At the
least this requires a projection of the accomplishments
to be expected in the technical area and an estimate of
the objectives our society will adopt over this time span.
This latter task requires something more than a demo-
graphic model of the future and a GNP projection year by
year for a decade or two.

At the least a guess must be made at the direction
where our shifting social values will take us, at what
rate, and with what consequences. On the map of the economic and social terrain so plotted it is the job of the
executive management to judge the range of potential lines
of corporate development that will open, what advantages
and obstacles each is likely to present, which direction
the firm's resources, both present and prospective, are
best suited for, and what are the best means for achieving the goals so defined. One of the key factors in
arriving at these control decisions is the comparative
social advantage of each course and the ethical basis for
such determinations.

The ethical problems of day-to-day affairs are not
difficult to solve within the framework of long-term control decisions except in rare instances. The main danger
encountered in the management of day-to-day affairs arises

10

from the loss, in pursuing the immediate, of an awareness
of relatedness. Tunnel vision puts the objective and the
means for its accomplishment in sharp focus, but the pro-
tective function of peripheral vision is lost in the process. It is the first concern of operative management to
reach the specific objectives set for it or that it has
set for itself. It is a constant obligation of executive
management to monitor the external effects as well as the
internal consequences of the pursuit of the objectives
agreed upon to assure their continuing acceptability and
advantage to society as well as to the corporation.

This obligation constantly to maintain a sense of
social awareness, the responsibility for directional improvisation concurrent with the shifts in public objectives, and the burden of anticipating the emergence of
new value systems in the world at large, fall primarily
on the executive manager.

It is not the function of the businessman to create
a separate ethos, differing from that of his society. Improvement in this line ought to be the concern of the businessman in his individual role, but it is not of the essence of his economic function. It is his function to
maintain in his enterprise the ethical standards that our
society observes and to assist in the general effort to
advance those standards as new social aspirations indicate.

Clearly there is not a separate ethic for managers.
So our question is reduced to the dimension of applying
the general values of society to the particular conditions that managers face in discharging their functions.

Business discharges the economic function of creating and distributing goods and services in accordance
with public demand as expressed in the market or by governmental directive. The pressure of government may be
effectively exerted directly or indirectly. It is the
function of the manager to see or foresee demand, to de-
vise skillful means of meeting it with the least expendi-
ture of human and capital resources, to assemble and organize the people and capital needed for the task, and to
direct their effective use in production and distribution.
Obviously society requires that the manager do his task
well, for the sum of our social demands substantially ex-
ceeds the productive capability of the resources at our
disposal. His own professional sense of public obligation inclines him in that direction. And the pressures
of the competitive market compel him to those ends.

Under these conditions the establishment and continuance in a venturesome course require courage and commitment of the executive group determined "to organize a future with a difference."

Where the fortunes and futures of others are involved, the risks of business must be managed with the interests of all in mind. These are satisfied by the recurring definition of "the subjective human purposes" to which all are devoted, and by the constant effort assuring that the system as a whole is moving toward them. This process of "improvisation on a general sense of direction" may not rest on any mere speculative impulse. However imprecise it must by the nature of things be, it must be sustained by the strength of the individual conscience and personal integrity of the leadership.

I have mentioned that the corporate value system must have both an outward and an inward base. That is, the corporation must be receptive and responsive to external impulses, and it must be internally perceptive and responsible. Just so, the management that makes value choices for the corporation must also find ethical resources both within and without. Laws can require conformity to a minimum standard of conduct, but they cannot create integrity or an ethical system of values. Yet these last are qualities that the professional executive must embrace, and it is professional executives on whom the corporation must rely for decisions. While the tests by which we rise in management are not specifically ethical in content, the office of executive management is in itself from time to time a test of ethics. Fortunately, those who have proven themselves otherwise fit for the office usually have the capacity to meet this test as well.

APPLICATION

To this point I have acknowledged the obligation of the large business corporation to serve certain interests of employees, shareholders, government, the general public, and the many publics into which the general public divides. Business is not bound to serve every interest of each of these collectivities, but only those which coincide with the "public" interest. What the public interest is, where and how it manifests itself, and to what extent each group may claim its benefit by separate assertion are questions to which the answers are somewhat obscure.

I have pinned on those employees described as management the function of making the operational decisions which
affect all of those interests. And I have fixed on the
executive management the responsibility for setting the
policy guidelines controlling decisions of this sort and
for maintaining an appropriate level of sensitivity in all
areas of management to the public interests touching all
of these communities. The corporation also has its own
vital interests which, since the corporation is, as I have
said, affected with a public interest, are of the same
dignity. Therefore management is bound to see that the
interests of others are served in such a way that those
of the corporation are not disserved.

The engagement in dissertations on moral theory and
in declarations of ethical principle is exhilarating, edi-
fying, even euphoric, leaving the participant bedewed, in
consequence of his exertions, with the holy water of self-
righteousness. But specific matters in sweaty contention,
with their shifting issues, shifty facts, conflicting interests, and imperfectly applicable rules of decision are
something else. The irresponsible outsider can always reduce the terms of the contest to those simple elements related to the single principle that interests him. So he
sees the dispute as one between the powers of light and
darkness, where conscience points an obvious path to an
uncomplicated and definitive conclusion. But management
is not privileged to peel the artichoke in this fashion;
separate the issues it may, but it cannot dispense with
any. It must find a route that recognizes every interest
and arranges them in such balance that no community is
alienated and the enterprise can function effectively.

This, it may be argued, is a course of expedience
and not of ethics. But an ethic which answers problems
without composing differences is neither ethical nor ex-
pedient. The corporation is justified because it serves
the public interest by giving economic employment to
people and capital and by providing a continuous flow of
goods and services that are responsive to public need or
public demand. So a solution which satisfies an ethical
postulate but which defeats the corporate function is
fatally deficient from every viewpoint, including the
ethical.

Hence the manager's theatre of action rarely offers
opportunity for the isolated abstract consideration and
disposition of an issue on strictly ethical grounds. Discovering the point of balance among conflicting or inharmonious claims is his ordinary pursuit. Further, these
interests are never static, and their point of rest is

13

always shifting. So the manager is not only denied the clerical ecstasy of banishing sin and proclaiming virtue's triumph, but he cannot even enjoy the temporal pleasure of "solving" the problem. His is the unending job of managing it. He is bound to reflect with amusement or bitterness, as he responds to the public pressures of the day, that the pursuit of happiness for all is not disposed to advance the quality of justice for any. For the requirement that he act in the public interest forbids his resort to a dispassionate impartiality in judgment and demands of him inveterate discrimination by reason of person or circumstance.

The general sense of direction around which consensus is obtained and plans are formulated receives its focus from the constant necessity to increase the skill and capital resources of the firm and the twin necessity to increase the production output of all the resources of the firm. Growth in production and in productivity are tests which every ethically admirable solution must satisfy or it fails, and probably on ethical grounds. Those weary of the stretching demands of living urge that these are choices, not necessities, and choices motivated by greed for profit or power or both. This answer will always satisfy those who think in small dimensions and cherish the miniature conclusions that they permit.

Ethical judgments may legitimately appeal to an ideal, but it must be an ideal rooted in reality. To appraise conduct according to standards founded in a world that never was may be within the realm of poetic license, but it certainly falls outside the scope of an ethical commission. Fair criticism of managerial performance must invoke the same context as that which enveloped the actions under appraisal. So the test is not whether a particular public interest is advanced to perfection, but whether the sum of the interests with which that certain interest is involved was nurtured in commendable or objectionable fashion.

2

PERSPECTIVES ON CORPORATE MANAGEMENT RESPONSIBILITY

INTERNAL OR EXTERNAL ETHICAL STANDARDS?

<u>Anthony W. Connole</u>: I would assert at the beginning that
business management constitutes important leadership in
our society today, and that the role of leaders is to
lead, not just in economics, but in matters relating to
civic, ethical, and moral matters within our economic society.

I found Mr. Hanold's paper to contain repeated emphasis on the role of management as one of ascertaining and
forecasting society's desires and then striking a balance
among the competing interests in order to gain acceptability from the society in which it operates. He describes
the management's theater of action as discovering the
point of balance among conflicting or inharmonious claims.

The only reference made to finding ethical resources
from within is described by Mr. Hanold as a personal conscience modified by external expectations. Again, the
modification of reacting to what others desire of you,
rather than internally generating an independent set of
ethical standards.

I would have preferred more emphasis on the obligation to provide ethical leadership from within the conduct
of the business. I don't derogate the need also to find
actions acceptable to the general society in which you operate. It is a matter of emphasis.

My second critical comment is on the theory that the
computer has introduced professionalism and therefore a
different ethic into business management. It is true
that there are many professional disciplines in management
today, but most of them, in my experience, blend into the

total situation of the corporation that they find upon their arrival rather than make some kind of effort to change it as a result of different views or ethical standards. As a matter of fact, the computer and the human professionals who control it often are used in further defense of corporate activities under attack in our society.

This is an age of specialization in industry, and each specialist handles his own specialty. Unfortunately, no one ends up being a specialist in the ethical aspects of business activity.

I am intrigued with a question which was hardly dealt with in any depth: Can a multinational corporation, particularly in the highly nationalistic world we live in, make a social investment to meet multinational concepts of needs? It is a very complex situation because different views as to society's needs can generate from one nation to another, and Mr. Hanold's paper places great emphasis on reading the pulse of society and reacting to it. In a situation like that, the question becomes one of whose pulse you read. Do you read and then balance precariously between all of the pulses? Mr. Hanold makes the apparent presumption throughout the paper that no change is needed, that the present structure and the present methods of management are adequate to deal with the many challenging criticisms that are being leveled against industry today.

A question very centrally posed is: Can a corporation in search of profits make a proper social investment sufficient to prevent society from imposing its will through legislation?

Kirk O. Hanson: Mr. Hanold said that corporate policies, and not ethics, dictate many of the things that we are referring to today as expressions of corporate responsibility.

We must think about the whole development of corporate policies that are in the social welfare. There are types of issues where there is no way the corporation can justify public interest action, action in the social welfare, given their focus upon increase of profitability. It is hard to tell a multinational corporation that it should maximize the benefit to the less developed countries in which it is operating if it has the ability to bargain for a much better situation within those nations. It is hard to tell all business that a no-growth philosophy is one that they should support.

Without the individual businessman making a commitment to some sort of overriding ethical approach, some kind of overriding ethical standard, the corporation will continue to be a hindrance, hardly any help, to social welfare.

HOW MUCH POWER DOES MANAGEMENT WIELD?

James E. Lee: Clearly the need exists for ventilation and resolution of the issues of corporate responsibility in the social and ecological field. We remind ourselves that management has a responsibility to its shareholders, its employees, and the consuming public. Yet how many of us are wise enough to be consistently equitable to all three parties when many decisions cut across the interests of two parties, if not all three?

I say this because there is a widespread misconception about the degree to which managers actually shape corporate activities. Businessmen who manage a large company with great physical assets have much less power than is usually ascribed to them. Every decision that must be implemented somewhere down the chain of command must be implemented by a person or by people, and action results not by command but by persuasion. Let me give you an example. Top management can have the greatest personal commitment to specific goals under the Equal Employment Opportunity Program. Yet how does such top management get such goals implemented in a plant in Louisiana through three or four layers of command? Not by an executive order but by persuasion.

My point is that in an organization where the chain of command is long and managers manage people rather than paper or physical plants, power is largely mythical.

Donald F. McHenry: Does this modesty about the power of management go too far? I want to dissent here.

Mr. Lee states that you don't get things done by executive order but by persuasion. Others have said, "Not directives but guidelines." I think clearly it is both of these things. We saw in the Eisenhower Administration this same approach to civil rights--"We are going to work it out in the hearts of people, the hearts of men." We all know what happened. Nothing.

There is a need for persuasion, but persuasion has to be accompanied by very, very clear conclusions and sometimes pretty strong directives. I have gone through American corporations in South Africa and have talked with people down the line in management. Where the top management was taking a very clear stance about what was wanted done in the way of human relations and improving the status of employees, action was evident. It was also clear in instances where this had not been done. One met a whole long line of rationalization.

I am not saying that it is possible simply to give an order and expect that the order is going to be carried out. I think that Eisenhower discovered that government wasn't like the military. He could not give an order and have it carried out. I am saying that it is a combination of both the directive and persuasion. If we think that persuasion alone is going to do it, we are fooling ourselves.

Raymond Bauer: The question is then: How much initiative should the businessman or business leader take? I would submit that there is a limit to the amount of initiative that we want him to take, because to the extent that he runs ahead of the pack, he can run only guided by his own values and his own sense of what is right.

I think we have been spending quite a few decades trying to keep the business community from doing exactly that. Some point of balance is obviously called for.

Mr. Hanson: I think that any kind of presumption that we can have businessmen as a neutral force in the society is false. It is not a question of whether businessmen begin to use their power, informal and formal, for certain kinds of social goals with which we might not agree. We cannot somehow neutralize the behavior of American businessmen to the point where they are not taking any kind of action for or against particular kinds of social objectives. Power is exercised one way or the other, and I would rather be concerned with trying to encourage what I would term the ethical use of that power. Trying to figure out some way to hold back the power of business is a hopeless quest.

Roger F. Murray: I really wonder whether the large, modern, public corporation in itself is likely or can be expected to generate strong ethical standards and principles. Is not this whole process of management designed for this kind of participation? Perhaps we should not anticipate that in dealing with our difficult complicated issues the modern publicly-held corporation will in fact ever take a clear, explicit, firm stand; and we should recognize that the very process of arriving at a consensus will involve degrees of compromise along the way. We won't get either the clarity or the firmness of stance that sometimes I think we are looking for.

We are perhaps looking for the kinds of action that a corporation dominated by a single individual in an authoritarian manner could deliver. We know of such companies largely in historical terms. There is no longer a General

Johnson running J&J. There is no longer the elder Henry
Ford. There is no longer a large number of these personal-
ities who ran companies in which an individual laid down
the law.

　　The relevance of this, it seems to me, is that it
should perhaps condition our expectations of the modern
corporation.

<u>Stephen B. Farber</u>: I think for analytical purposes we
have to be very careful about determining in our own minds
precisely what the range of management options really is.
The extent to which managers in fact do enjoy freedom in
making decisions of consequence, whether on environmental
matters or minority hiring or whatever else, is subject,
to some degree, to government policy. The suggestion of
progress in civil rights after the Eisenhower era is a
clear example of that. Any manager can tell you how various civil rights laws have directly affected operations.

　　Obviously there is a great deal of latitude beyond
what the laws may require. The whole foreign investment
question is an example. When Gulf Oil decided that it
would go into Angola, it didn't really have to consult ex-
tensively with the United States Government, even though
the United States Government during this period did not
support what was going on in Angola. In decisions of this
kind managers have a great range of options. It is very
important that we be clear where the options exist and
where they do not.

　　A second question is: What decisions should managers
make themselves and what decisions should they share with
others?

THE CONCEPT OF "PROFESSIONAL MANAGEMENT"

<u>Charles W. Powers</u>: To the extent we use the word "pro-
fessional," with all the concepts surrounding that word,
we build in an understanding of a man or woman who is
willing to use his or her own conscience in the context
of a number of competing claims, and move in a very specific direction. As we use the word "professional," we
use a concept different from "manager," "responder," or
"arbiter."

　　The concept of professional suggests a very strong
element of decision in the discretionary space where one
has power. We justify the existence of that space not on
the ground that there must be room for balancing interests,

19

but on the grounds that for skill and competence to be wedded with consideration of the public interest, arenas for discretionary judgment are required. Much of what we have seen in the corporate responsibility debate in the last couple of years can be looked at from this interesting perspective, namely, that many of the targets of advocate groups in environment matters, in minority hiring, and in practices of multinational corporations really stem from the fact that people holding certain views have not been successful in getting governmental policies in these fields to be consistent with their views. There are, then, two questions before us. First, to what extent do executive leaders of large corporations have the arenas for discretionary judgment normally possessed by professionals? Second, is the public interest generally served better by increasing or decreasing the scope of their "professional" influence?

Timothy Smith: Who is going to bring up the ethical questions? People in management are not likely to bring up such issues as the employment of women or sexist advertising in as vocal and as strident a way as the women's group that feels that this is a very personal and serious issue for them. The depth of meaning and the depth of understanding of an issue comes very much from one's personal relation to it.

Mr. Hanold made reference to "expertise" in the job of directing. What does expertise in directing mean in 1973? Does it mean how to read a balance sheet and having a businessman's savvy to bring his corporation to a better profit level for 1974?

Does it mean, in the case of General Motors, bringing on the Board of Directors someone like Dr. Sullivan, who I don't think was brought on because he could read that balance sheet? Though I am sure he can read it, he wasn't brought on because he could read it better than anyone else in that room. He was brought on because he had a contribution to make that came from a specific nurturing and learning in the black community.

Patricia C. Sexton: I would like to say, based on the kinds of things that I have heard here, that I am not very optimistic that corporations are moving in ethical directions, and I would like to see a lot of legislation myself. I see that management does respond, as General Motors is responding, to auto pollution problems due to legislation and not through great interest in them as human problems.

<u>Jon P. Gunnemann</u>: It strikes me that we really have had
three different kinds of questions in this discussion. I
will try to deal with them.

The first are questions of management, questions about
how corporate managers think. Here it is helpful to make
a distinction between descriptive and normative thinking,
between discussing what is and what ought to be.

Just a word about the descriptive discussion that went
on. Terry Hanold's paper was a description of what the
manager is about. He was trying to make the point that the
modern manager is in some way freer than the entrepreneur
was in dealing with ethical issues. Now to say that he is
free is probably a bit misleading, but the suggestion was
that, because of a shift in the kind of decision-making
processes within the corporate structure, he is freer in
some ways to focus on normative issues than the entrepreneur was.

There was a claim made by a corporate manager that the
buck stops there. In one way, this is a very strong statement. On the other hand, we were warned that the type of
freedom that the manager has in these new processes is a
freedom which permits him to <u>manage</u> rather than <u>solve</u>
problems.

On the normative side, there was some disagreement
about how much power management ought to have. Here I
have three different kinds of questions, still part of the
total first question about management. First, how much
and what kind of power should managers have? To some extent this is obviously dependent upon the factual description, but it can be put in the form of a question that also
becomes normative. Second, depending upon the kind of
power he has, do you really want him to be making ethical
decisions of one sort or another? For example, do you
want him to be setting or generating ethical standards?
Do you want him to be making decisions according to those
standards?

Then the third question, which really follows from
the second: Do you really want leadership from management
formulating standards, or do you only want something like
a balancing of interests, a kind of responsiveness to what
is going on out there and attentiveness to the norms being
generated by society, demands being made by society, and
so on?

Clearly the answers to these questions depend to some
extent on your factual analysis, the kind of power that

21

the management actually has, but I think it can be dealt with independently of factual analysis. That is the first set of questions, questions about management itself.

Lurking behind the question about how corporate management thinks is another kind of question that was being raised: Is there some kind of fundamental incompatibility between the interests of a business organization and ethical demands? There is an implicit suggestion in this question that merely reading the pulse of society at large will not work, or that it will not be enough, or that the reading of the pulse will in some way always be an interpretative reading, interpreted by management according to its own processes.

The point was made that the balancing of interests in itself is not enough because some kinds of ethical demands will upset the balancing ledger of any manager. That is, you can play the game of balancing competing claims to a point, but there are some kinds of claims that managers could not, if they met them all, balance. The point made is that there is a difference between policy and ethics, and the latter, ethical choices, sometimes require more than just hard decisions. Ethical choices are frequently hard choices, but, borrowing from existentialist language, they are sometimes tragic decisions. The concept of the manager balancing competing claims tends to ignore the possibility that some kinds of moral demands simply cannot be balanced within the average corporate ledger.

This then raises a third type of problem and brings us back full circle to how corporate management thinks. That is, is the manager's self-image about what he is doing "wrong" in some way? Is it possible that his self-image is not necessarily coincident with the image held of him by persons not in the managerial class?

The managers in our discussion give the impression that they assume there is a sort of beneficent judging of competing claims which in a total process will ultimately work out best for everybody. But there are other persons in the discussion who suggested that this balancing of claims neither was nor could be so harmonious. They suggest that you really do have at times a hard conflict of interests that will be resolved according to which interest has the greater concentration of power behind it. What you most frequently have is a conflict situation rather than a harmonious process situation.

This then raised the question of whether you don't need more than a simple managerial process or information process. Possibly one needs a third party of some sort.

Now you can conceive of this in two ways. You can conceive of it as an adversary or conflict situation, the interest of the corporation versus the interest of other groups. Or you can conceive of it as a situation where persons in an advisory capacity provide a third standpoint that seeks to correct the managerial self-image and managerial self-understanding, as well as those of other competing groups. In this instance, what kind of advisory body or third party should there be?

In summary, we are left with a number of perplexing questions. By what method might corporate managements be aided or encouraged to exercise more socially responsive leadership? Given their relative independence from ownership control, given the fact that they do have some power, how much power do you want corporate management to exercise?

Is responsive or responsible management simply a process that balances competing claims? Or are there some kinds of standards that can be generated? Where and how do you generate these standards for business? Is there a conflict of interests between the demands of ethics and the processes of business?

PRINCIPLES: THE CORPORATE
SOCIAL AUDIT

It is generally acknowledged that corporate social responsibility means little without some manner or procedure for sorting out areas of social concern and measuring corporate performance in areas of social concern. Indeed the difficulty of defining the corporate manager's proper role illustrated in the previous chapter stems in part from uncertainty both inside and outside the corporation about the real social impact of large economic institutions.

A manuscript (soon to be published) by Raymond A. Bauer and Dan H. Fenn, Jr., entitled The Corporate Social Audit, was made available to the participants prior to the conference and generated a wide-ranging discussion of the manner in which the impact of corporate activity upon society might be evaluated. Bauer and Fenn write:

> Ralph Nader, consumerism, ecology, minority problems, women's liberation, South Africa, misleading advertising, Campaign GM, student and church activism all tumbled over one another seeking attention, to the point where the businessman of the 70's is caught up in a confusing turbulence of demands and charges and concerns, all marching under the umbrella of "social responsibility." In a time of public disaffection . . . [a] . . . changed—or, better, rearranged—value structure and the emergence of new tools to enforce it are now impacting on the American corporation.
>
> The need for some sort of criteria for the social responsibility of business, some kind of definition of just what the words mean, some tools for measuring performance against this definition, has now become a matter of real urgency. The social activists need a definition which is generally accepted if they are to make their charges viable; if they are to "improve" corporate performance, they need something more than a vague and subjective notion of what is

"good" and a loose method of accounting.
If the corporate executives are to "improve" their performance in this field,
they too need to know what the "field"
is. Even if they simply want to protect
themselves from the complaints of customers and activists, they need such a
definition.

The term that has come to stand for such performance
measurement is "social audit," a recent addition to the
burgeoning corporate social responsibility vocabulary.
In complete form, perhaps, the corporate social audit
would permit firms to report their performance on issues
of current social concern with the same regularity that
they report financial performance. However, as the Bauer
and Fenn work demonstrates, the difficulty of developing
a comprehensive and objective evaluation of the social
performance of corporations on a continuing basis is becoming patently clear. Indeed, this book can be viewed
as a compendium of "approaches with crippling defects,"
amply illustrated by case studies.

Still, these two writers bring some order out of the
whirlwind. They indicate that current conceptions of the
social audit fall into four categories. The most modest
approach is simply to collect information that a company
is not committing "social injury," or is not under indict-
ment by a government body. The second relies on the im-
pressions of knowledgeable and concerned people who have
collected some data. A third approach is to take selected
areas of corporate activity and review them in detail. An
example of this approach is found in the work of the Council on Economic Priorities, which has devised a methodology
for assessing a corporation's impact on water pollution,
comparing it to other corporations in the same industry,
and reporting on it. The fourth approach attempts to develop sophisticated quantitative measures of social responsibility and to put them on balance sheets.

The discussion in Chapter 3, which begins with a
brief summary presentation by Mr. Bauer, indicates considerable participant skepticism that a shared definition
or viable methodology for a social measurement process
worthy of the word "audit" is imminent or even possible.
In addition to the obvious questions, "Can performance in
social areas really be measured?" and "What counts as a
societal contribution?" there arose an even more basic
one: Can a pluralistic society with competing and often

incompatible norms and mores produce a common understanding of what is socially desirable? And even if it can, how is that understanding to be related to the overseas operations of a multinational corporation operating in several dramatically different cultural contexts?

Chapter 4 seeks to highlight the debate on a related question, "Who is the social auditor?" Viewpoints varied as to whether the audit should be "in house," and thus primarily for corporate management and internal corporate consumption only, or "public," and thus for external disclosure. As the effort to construct a methodology for corporate social auditing goes on, one fact seems clear from the discussion: The continuing pressure from groups external to corporate management is at least making "in house" audits more likely.

3

THE CORPORATE SOCIAL AUDIT: WHAT IS IT?

Raymond Bauer: The concept of the corporate social audit has had fairly good currency since 1971. It has been called "The Great What-Is-It." Most people find it very difficult to understand what it is, and I cannot give a single descriptive statement other than to say that it is a social balance sheet. If you ask me what a social balance sheet is, I cannot describe it.

In General Motors, it is said that the public policy committee performs an auditing function. Now if the name of the game is to make an assessment of social performance, then the public policy committee does it. It does not do it in the form of an elaborate procedure for gathering data where everything has to be performance-measured, nor can you get close analyses that balance out. Yet it does perform a useful function in assessing what General Motors is up to.

Given some of the technical difficulties, my advice to people has been to try to avoid the profound questions and to do something that would be useful at this point in time that will enable management to learn how to keep "social score" on the company.

On the whole, most companies want to do it internally, at least at first, which is a sensible posture. I have suggested as a first stage that companies try to figure out some manageable working package by concentrating on the explicitly social programs the company has.

What activities are you in that you would not be in for regular business purposes? It turns out that there are many companies that cannot answer that right off the bat. They have to do a large scrutiny job, for such information is not readily assembled. In addition to not being assembled, there often is not one single person who knows where to look for it.

This first step in gathering an inventory has been proven useful in a fair number of companies. I have had people say that it is not a social audit. I would only say that the inventory is a starting point, and then you ought to go back and think. If you have developed the skill and the ability to collect that inventory for your company, you have some information about what you have been doing that you did not have previously. The next step is to look at costs. It is a policy question as to whether or not at this particular stage you do want to probe around and even get the out-of-pocket costs assembled, because they usually have not been assembled before.

The real question is, however, can you measure performance? It is sometimes very, very difficult to get measures of performance. It depends upon what you are trying to measure. With this in mind, we have suggested a process audit which aims at the best description of the program you can arrive at, where you can get intermediate performance measures and sufficient description. Somebody who is informed can look at it and say, "Yes, these people are doing pretty well," or "No, they are not doing very well."

Robert M. James: I will confine my remarks to a few basic observations. The first is that any audit of any sort has to make some basic assumptions: First, that we know what we want in the way of social programs; second, that we know what we want to obtain from the audit; and third, that we clearly want to establish credibility. In trying to decide what we want, it seems to me that one of the most important things to recognize is that the businessman cannot live in a vacuum. He is truly of the society in which he is imbedded.

I would like to focus on one point which, for me, and I may assume for the rest of you, is one that is going to be increasingly vexing. This is the international scope of business today in the midst of a whole series of separate regional, ideological, and ethical structures. I think that any of us engaged in international business or close to an international business realizes that a policy may sound fine for application in the United States but by the time you go very far beyond the borders of this country you have increasing difficulty in trying to interpret that policy and find a meaningful way of using it.

Also in this connection we need to take into account that the international businessman, the multinational businessman, can be as ethical as possible only as long as he stays in business. In many cases the aspects of his competitor, particularly where that competitor is multinationally based, and some of the basic social structures, may have a set of values different from that set which he would use in setting up his own policies.

I am not trying to suggest in any sense that we want to try to favor American business. That is not the point. The point is, whenever an American businessman tries to use his ethical system, he has to keep in mind, when he finds himself in other social areas, that he may find other ethical patterns at work. We need to know what we want before we can truly begin to talk about auditing. We need to recognize in many cases that we are operating not in one value system, and not even in one social order, but in many.

In conclusion, I think to expect a great deal from social auditing initially would be leaving ourselves open to a great deal of disappointment. There is little structure that anyone can discern at the moment considered appropriate for efforts in trying to measure or report in an audit sense. The agent of audit or the auditor is anything but clear. We can push the analogy of the financial audit too far. Setting aside the meaning of audit in the financial sense, what we need to recognize is that what we are really trying to say is that someone settled on a policy, laid out a course of action, and started to do something about it. We would like to know what has been done, how far it has gone, what the process is, and what the results have been. Whatever that may be, we want it done by someone who is sufficiently disinterested to be impartial, and sufficiently qualified to be believable.

WHAT DOES CORPORATE RESPONSIBILITY MEAN?

Charles Powers: I think the key question is: What in the world does corporate responsibility mean? There is no definition of corporate responsibility that is widely recognized. Given that, many people are forced to rely for indicators upon the market mechanism, government regulations, or the pushing and pulling among various parts of the society.

I would like to suggest that there is one possible starting point for an internal audit that might give it considerably greater clarity and a base on which to build. It rests upon the basic distinction which Jon Gunnemann, John Simon, and I make in The Ethical Investor between the negative injunction that we all share not to do harm to others and the affirmative duty to try to go out and do good in the world. To put that in a different way, there is, on the one hand, an obligation we all have, within the things we are already doing, not to be hurting people. That obligation is distinguishable from a desire to develop programs that go out and look for good things to do. I realize that it does not clarify very much to limit yourself to the former, but at least it cuts down the range of things managers will have to look at within an internal corporate audit.

Then I would suggest that you follow us in our book one step further. Look at the public policy norms, particularly those that relate to health, safety, and basic freedoms, and try to get a hold on those values as expressed in international and domestic law that impinge on the various aspects of your business. Now admittedly, as soon as you have said domestic and international law, you have opened up all the questions that Bob James has been pushing at us. You will have to take health, safety, and the basic freedoms concerns on down to their application in actual statutes. Here, as you begin to try to apply them to various divisions of your corporation, the conflicts immediately get worse. Nevertheless, my point is that if a corporation is trying to operate generally within the confines of the law or morals of society, it may help to look to international law and domestic law at the level of general health, safety, and freedoms, and to find at least some enduring or basic ideas about what the world community has said it wants to establish for its common life. When you get into the various value conflicts, you at least know what they are with respect to any particular area in which the corporation operates.

It seems to me that if you went through a process of sorting out basic public policy norms and looked at each division within your corporation, you would see where they do or do not impinge on your business. Then the job would be to test out what you are doing in those areas. You would have at least one aspect of an audit that you could use internally to test your own experience in addition to that of the manager's individual conscience. You would not try, in the first place at least, to test in a wholly impossible way all of the total social impacts of your operation. And you would certainly not do what Ray

Bauer proposes, i.e., concentrate attention on your "good guy" programs.

I am assuming that in fact most of the internal audits of this type would not initially be made public, desirable as that might be. I am also assuming that, realistically, managers will find it impossible at first to allow groups outside the corporation itself to have access even to all of the information that would make these audits inside the company decisive or viable.

This is not as great a loss as it might first appear, since investors--and other "publics" for that matter-- should not expect that audits of this type would provide sufficient data for judging the overall goodness or badness of any corporation. I doubt that anyone outside the corporation can make overall performance judgments. If public constituencies of the corporation wish to have impact, they must pick out either particular areas where they feel they have some knowledge about the social harm the corporation is doing or some area of affirmative work they wish the corporation to move into.

External constituencies will and should be pressing the corporation on those particular issues about which they know, and hopefully corporations will be prepared to disclose the data relevant to those issues. The near-term difficulties cf the social audit movement would, I hope, make the corporation manager sensitive to the fact that when people or groups do pick out particular issues and do raise them up, they are not making, nor can they make, overall judgments about corporations--they are not saying, "Overall, General Motors is a good thing or a bad thing." Instead, managers should be aware that such groups are simply saying, sometimes with passion, "Certain aspects of General Motors' activities are worth looking at more carefully." In other words, I am suggesting that if the complete social audit is a distant dream, then the fact that a group picks out only particular issues is precisely what should be expected of those who stand outside the corporation. In the interim that precedes full social disclosure the push and pull on specific issues will and should continue.

Byron E. Grant: I have a question or two. I cannot find any particular objection in my own mind here to the idea of a social audit, or whatever you want to call it--a social audit, a corporate social investigation, or something else. What I am trying to decide is whether or not my own company is doing the kind of things that you are talking about.

33

For a number of years our annual report has included what is being done on safety and what is being done in pollution control, and also how much money is being spent for these purposes. For instance, there is an announcement now of another five-year program of $100 million to be spent over five years. What is being done in this whole area? Is that what we are talking about, or how is it different from that?

Again, if you wanted some information and you came to me and asked for it, what is it that I would have to send other than that type of thing which includes salary surveys, hiring surveys, minority groups, etc.? What should I present?

Mr. Bauer: I think that if that were presented, you would be fully responsive. Very few companies are prepared to be that responsive. Yet did you provide a definable, capable domain you were covering so that people could know what you might have left out? It is possible that people could look at your list and say, "I can't imagine why I would be interested in those dollar figures." Frequently there is an almost complete absence of norms.

Robert S. Potter: Mr. Grant does not seem to have any problem sharing information, and yet his president, Mr. Frank Milliken, when I called him and asked him for some information about mining copper in Puerto Rico, would not even see us. Yet we had in one little fund 10,000 shares of his company.

The response we made to that rebuke was to get together some people and go down to Puerto Rico to hold a public hearing. We got the information. I suggest that if this information is not forthcoming and the audit is not a feasible mechanism internally to some extent, what is the option? It seems that if a company is doing a good job, you can get information. If they are not doing a good job, you are not going to get the information.

Mr. Grant: I would not try to determine what Mr. Milliken said, but I would say that as far as Puerto Rico is concerned, we don't have an operation there. This is something that is planned for the future, an investment in the future. You cannot pronounce very well on a social audit type of thing what you do on an operation that does not exist.

Mr. Potter: I beg to differ with you. You have a joint venture there with Amex, and you have mining rights.

Mr. Grant: We have that. It is still not much of a going concern in the corporation.

Mr. Potter: That is what we were questioning; whether it should become a going concern because of the manner and the terms of the negotiations. We finally learned about these problems from the government in Puerto Rico, since the companies would not disclose them. This, in part, has brought a suspension of the negotiations, because the old question of ecology came up as well as the whole question of the rights of the Puerto Ricans themselves. Not only is it their own property, but mining there has effects on the island itself. This process took a hell of an investment in time.

Mr. Grant: There is again more than one party involved in this. Sometimes in a case like that a company is not actually at liberty to speak its will when there are other parties involved, particularly on something that, as I have said, is not a going concern in the corporation.

Mr. Potter: Amex is very much open. They have a 50 percent interest, and you still have a 50 percent ownership. We did not get information from your company, so we had to go down to Puerto Rico and get it.

Mr. Grant: I am glad you did. We don't have it. Perhaps you can give it to us.

THE PROBLEMS OF PERFORMANCE MEASUREMENT

Jon Gunnemann: It seems to me that we have different things in mind when we talk about the kind of social responsibility that might be susceptible to some kind of quantification and performance measurements.

Rather than calling this concept a social audit, I will call it a performance measurement. The notion of any kind of performance measurement assumes that you do have some type of goal that you can measure up to, and there are certain actions which are more in character, which do admit of that type of analysis.

There are other kinds that don't admit such analysis. There are times when you have a genuine conflict of interest; a moral issue arises because you have a real disagreement about an ethical issue. You are caught in a position where there is no way to measure performance unless you measure the ability of management to handle this

kind of conflict. It strikes me as very difficult to do.
I don't know how you could quantify that.

There are managements that are obviously very good,
and others that shy away from it and run in the other direction. It seems to me that one of the things that people
have said here is that they are worried about the second
kind of area--that is, conflict of interest--an area where
either we don't know what we want or where to go for norms.

As Bob James was saying, we often have two competitive
ethical systems--different ethical systems where you have
something amounting not to a performance problem but to a
political process. There has to be some kind of bargain,
a give-and-take compromise. I think that an auditing process or a measuring process cannot deal with this give-
and-take. These are procedural problems which require the
establishment of internal house procedures, or something
of this sort, to handle them.

I have listed a few areas in which different issues
arise, and have indicated how they are affected by different kinds of norms.

First, there are moral problems that arise for which
we have very clear public norms to guide us. For instance,
we have laws covering minority employment, equal employment opportunity, and pollution. These laws provide norms
that corporations have to measure up to. In this area the
corporation can probably engage in a performance evaluation of its own. You have very clearly designated goals,
and indications of where you have to go.

In addition to these public norms provided by law,
there is a second area where you can be fairly certain
about what you are doing with certain kinds of informal
norms. For example, a company can probably to some extent
quantify the social cost of its operations to the town in
which it is located. It can also quantify the positive
contributions it is making to the town.

In the third kind of situation, moral problems arise
because you have competing norms. In this area there is
no longer a question of measurement of the performance.
A classic case of competing norms is where companies are
being asked on the one hand to produce a pollution-free
automobile, which they apparently can do through the use
of platinum, a material the securing of which involves en-
gaging in an activity in South Africa that could be con-
strued as violating a different kind of public norm, namely, a United Nations mandate about doing business with
that government.

There is a fourth situation, one in which you have a norm but you have no sanction. For example, the United States has voted on certain things in the United Nations, yet does not enforce these in the regulation of corporate operations overseas.

A fifth area exists in which you simply have no norms at all. A situation like this would arise if an oil company decided to go into a Middle Eastern country to develop oil wells there and received a concession but a group of stockholders objected for political or moral reasons. Here you don't have any kind of clearly defined public norms. All you have is the case of some people who differ in their interpretation of the proper policy.

Finally, there is the international situation where the conflict lies between local norms and the norms of the home society.

In some of the cases I have outlined, the norms problem is not very difficult. They are there to be used, and then what you need is not the result of the norms but generation of information to find out whether you are meeting them. In other cases you do have a number of problems: competing norms, no norms, or norms without sanction.

Dr. James: As a group we may need to begin to think about what kinds of things we should expect to get factual information on in a consistent manner on some sort of a periodic basis where that is possible. I think again that we have had several indications of what this might be. EEO reports show some compliance with pollution regulation, employment, and safety, etc. It seems to me that there is probably a great deal of information, good, hard, factual information, that does not depend upon conflicting value judgments. These EEO statements simply report the information and let the reader decide whether it is good or bad. If we were really trying to get started, this would be one way to do it.

4

WHO IS THE
SOCIAL AUDITOR?

AN IN-HOUSE OR PUBLIC AUDIT?

<u>Timothy Smith</u>: Whom is the audit for? If it is an in-
house document, then it is obviously a private document.
The Equal Employment Opportunity form was mentioned. What
if a group of churches, foundations, or concerned individual stockholders ask for this information to be displayed
and shared with them, whether confidentially or publicly?
They go to General Motors or American Can and say, "Could
we have this information? Could you put it out in front
of us because we think it is important for us to have the
information to evaluate adequately whether you are the
kind of corporation and whether you are doing the kind of
job we are satisfied with." What kind of reasoning would
be at work in a company's unwillingness to share such information? Why would this not be a perfectly natural
thing to put in front of all stockholders if they were interested, and to have the social audit, if we are still
going to use the term, on this very specific thing, which
we all agree is a priority issue? What is the problem
with having a shared specific issue social audit about
which the public knows?

<u>Charles Judd</u>: I think that Mr. Bauer has done one real
service by illustrating that in making any kind of an
audit, if we can still use that word, it is very hard, almost impractical, to try to employ the same concepts that
are utilized in financial audits.
     Maybe if we start to think in other terms and then
look at some of the things that have been done, we can

focus on the value of this kind of inventory for either internal or external use. For instance, safety, which we have not heard too much about and which is one of the real social issues: Practically all firms keep safety records. These are usually required by insurance companies, and in some states, such as New York, they are required by law. Should these kinds of ratings be made public? That is a legitimate question that we must face.

Charles Powers: I would like to pick up something Bob James raised.

You seem to indicate, Bob, that we would be in a lot of difficulty in coming to a theoretical determination of norms in corporations that are operating cross-culturally, and seem to argue that this was not going to be important because some competitors would force you, by virtue of the competitive situation you would be in, away from those norms anyhow. Is that all there is to it, or do you have further thoughts on that?

Robert James: That is a difficult question to answer. Mike Goodfield says that by and large, unless and until society provides sufficiently understood levels of normally acceptable behavior it has the power to enforce, he suspects that you will always find those who are taking advantage of an unclear or soft situation, one way or another. This is my concern with norms. I think you truly need to try to understand what you can or cannot do with them.

We are a little bit presumptuous if we think we can begin to establish the norms here. I suspect that more powerful interests in our society will work their will on whatever may become obvious in a fuller disclosure of information, and begin to set their own norms through negotiations. This is probably a far more enduring and useful way in which it should be done.

I would much prefer to start with just the simple hard facts, information we know is either available or can become available, and find ways of making sure that this is placed in the public's view, and placed there in verifiable ways that people can then begin to deal with.

THE DIFFICULTY OF "TRADE-OFFS"

Horace E. Gale: I would like to ask Dr. Bauer two questions about how he would handle trade-offs within a

company. Let us say you have reported an increase in minority employment, but at the same time you have increased
white unemployment. How is that fact reported? The second question is, how would you handle the act of closing a
plant because it is impossible to correct the pollution if
that closing at the same time removes a major employer
from a small community?

Raymond Bauer: I would personally answer both in the same
way. Let us assume that I were called in to work with a
company making an audit that addressed those questions.
My goals would be to display in front of management all of
the pertinent information, including, for example, minority hiring that resulted in some white unemployment.
There is no place to go at this point except to the judgment of management for the integration of those value conflicts. As far as I can see, that is basically management's problem. It becomes a public problem when it becomes public. Now this is one of the reasons we have
shied away from the notion of a weighing scheme of five
points for minority hiring, three points for minority sup-
pliers, and seven points for pollution control. That
would mean imposing on data a value scheme that was pulled
out of a hat. It would deprive other people of the opportunity of making judgments in terms of their own values.

WHO IS THE SOCIAL AUDITOR?

Richard B. Smith: My trouble with the term social audit
is the use of the word "audit." An audit assumes that
you have someone independent of the management itself doing the calculating. An auditor is an independent public
accountant. The management does not audit itself. The
second problem for me in the use of the term is that it
tries to build a financial balance which is just not present in the social system. I don't know how you can construct a social audit profile of a company if the main
problem of the company is pollution of rivers or the atmosphere. The company will defend itself by saying, "Well,
I have so many points because I have this much minority
employment." It is not at all responsive to the question.

Mr. Judd: What would happen, Mr. Loomis, if the federal
government issued a regulation that companies had to disclose certain items. Then they would have to, wouldn't
they?

Philip A. Loomis: I would think that the federal government will, and perhaps should, require certain items of
information to be disclosed.

    I would hope, however, that it would not attempt to
require the impossible overall balance thing that seems
to be the contemplated objective of social audit propon-
ents: so many points for pollution, and so many points
for minority hiring. Nor would it suggest that these be
reduced to dollars and cents except in an entirely different audit.

Philip W. Moore: I too have trouble with "audit." In
fact, I am not sure what the purpose of the social audit
is or to whom it is directed. You suggest that it is
directed, and properly so, internally to management.

    That is the purpose of an audit, to get to know the
whole picture. It can be addressed to the management as
an additional tool to make a judgment. Who cares?

    In effect it boils down to this. If an investor can
get the information he can then make his own evaluation,
depending on his own interests. I don't say that the
audit isn't serving an important function, but I think
there can be certain uniform standards set up for making
public certain kinds of what we are now calling social information. This information is useful not for auditing
or as a guide to management but to trigger a dynamic political process which will hopefully lead to more responsible corporations and institutions.

Robert W. Worcester: I would like to ask Mr. Bauer, Mr.
Loomis, or Mr. Smith if anyone has explored or considered
whether the various security analyst services which do
comment on many things--for example, on the management of
companies and their future growth and development--whether
such services could be asked to include comments about social aspects of corporate activities? Is this a possibility?

Mr. Loomis: I don't know whether management would provide them with sufficient data to make an informed judgment on this. However, they would be interested. I
think that within limits they could do something of this
kind. These analysts could find out whether the corporation is performing in a specific area, such as minority
hiring, in accordance with generally accepted standards,
particularly those which have become embodied in law. If
it is not, the analyst could estimate how much it would

41

cost to meet those standards. That is the type of disclosure I think can be agreed upon. I would question whether the security analysts in the present state of their art and experience are in a position to go much further than that and to express a judgment as to whether a corporation is doing all that it should do to improve the general quality of life. I don't think that this is the expertise they have or I have.

Mr. R. Smith: I think I would agree with that assessment as to security analysts. With most security analysts their bread and butter, and what they look to, is the projected earnings per share. They are only interested in ecology where the company is going to have to lay out funds, which may reduce its profitability through the end of the year or for the next year.

This is a limiting aspect of looking to financial analysts for social commentary. It is accentuated by a combination of two things too many investors look for: one is measuring investment performance in terms of instant appreciation, and the other is an assumption about the marketplace, complete liquidity.

If you are quite assured that you can get out of a particular security in six (or fewer) months, many investors feel there is no reason to stay with that particular company over a long period of time or through periods of high expense. It is a presumption of people dealing with questions of securities market structure that we must have a highly liquid and active market. One of the costs of these attitudes is, when employers of financial analysts are competing for investable funds, to veer toward short-term analyzing, the pricing of securities upon near-term earnings. I think it is unlikely that you would get a sufficiently long-range analysis from the typical working securities analyst to measure social costs. He will focus upon the performance phenomena, historical earnings per share, and projected earnings for the year. I have some doubts from the way that group is presently constituted that it is the one to look to at this time for substantial help in this regard.

Roger Murray: I was going to comment on Tim Smith's point about the availability of those reports. It is my understanding that while the Dreyfus group has had pretty good success in obtaining these reports, because of the size of the Dreyfus group of mutual funds, other organizations without that clout have been turned down, even though ostensibly the purpose of the inquiry was identical with that of the Dreyfus group.

ISSUES OF PUBLIC DISCLOSURE

Mr. T. Smith: I know investors have had trouble getting
information. I guess ultimately the pressure goes to the
SEC, which has the power to compel the production of information about public-owned corporations.

Robert Potter: In those situations where corporations do
disclose full information voluntarily, investors would
likely be the group to whom managers will give it first.
But I think that you are always going to have the problem
that when there is no corporate controversy corporations
will not voluntarily say damaging things about themselves.
I don't know anyone who voluntarily goes around telling
people about the types of problems they have. It is not
an expected thing. (Indeed, it is only through liability
and other penalties that the Securities and Exchange Commission might succeed in getting a corporation to disclose
even adverse financial results, let alone socially dubious
practices.) So if you cannot expect corporations to sup-
ply this information voluntarily, then I guess the next
step is the step that various groups have taken when they
have had interests in particular things.

   The Episcopal Church is interested in South Africa,
and other groups are interested in other data. There is
a lot of fussing and fretting, and eventually the corporations respond to that. Some of what you see is not in itself particularly pretty to look at, but I think it does
show that at least some corporations are doing the best
they can in certain circumstances.

   Then there is a third route, and that is some form
of governmental compulsion to provide information in this
area, but that can come only if you can establish two
things: first, some objective criteria for blatantly un-
acceptable practices about which the government can say,
"If you don't produce it, you can be penalized"; second,
data about practices that are less blatant but still highly questionable. Such data could be compared among all
firms in a particular industry. The aim of the social
audit, or whatever you want to call it, is to reach a
point where you can expect that some reasonable government will manage it.

   Short of that, no matter how high the morality of
the investor or any other collective interest, he is not
going to compel the production of the less obvious information. I am wondering, Mr. Loomis, if there is some continuing movement within SEC to look at the sort of things
we are discussing here.

Mr. Loomis: I think you have described the problem in its present status fairly accurately. We are still thinking about it. We have not advanced beyond the point that you described, that is, information which is financially significant, because, in part, some among us at the Commission, and all of industry, seem to feel that this is all we are authorized to ask for. Beyond that, there is the problem of what information should be required. The state of the art of financial analysis has advanced to the point where you can specify fairly clearly what is required, but even that is not what it should be. We are worried about that. Once you turn to other than financial aspects, it becomes exceedingly difficult to specify clearly the information that is required in such a way that it is enforceable by law.

To avoid the information being either inadequate or misleading, we must bear in mind that it is the disposition of the company to put its best foot forward. This occurs financially and otherwise--we catch them at it fairly easily in the financial field, but it is more difficult to do this in the social field. We are currently involved in litigation with one of the public interest law firms, which says that we are obligated to move more aggressively into this area, and we are not really quarreling with that basic thesis. Maybe that is one of the reasons I am here, to see if I can learn a little bit more about what people do want, and in what way it could be specified and justified to the business community, which is already inclined to feel that even what we have asked for is far too much.

Dr. Murray: I wanted to supplement the comments made about the church activities with a word or two about the world of higher education and its interest in the subject. A center for research and public interest investment issues is in the process of being founded.* The funding is reasonably well assured between foundations and with as many as 50 colleges and universities signing up for a year's support of this center, designed to produce the kinds of information needed for investment committees and financial committees of educational institutions to take positions and make up their minds on controversial issues.

----

*Dr. Murray is referring here to the Investor Responsibility Research Center established in December, 1972, in Washington, D.C.

This reflects, I think, the continued forward movement of that process by which educational institutions
have finally worked out a structure of internal decision-
making and of internal methods of dealing with these kinds
of issues not previously admitted to the meetings of the
investment committee. An increasing number of educational
institutions are going to make decisions; they are going
to take sides. They are not going to try to avoid this;
they are going to try to face up to it.

The purpose of this center will be to provide timely
and specific kinds of information on both sides of the
controversial proposal in a form that will enable the individuals, who are facing up to those decisions, to have
in hand the kinds of material that they need for arriving
at a judgment.

What this reflects, I think, is the fact that in the
world of higher education it has been recognized that
these kinds of concerns are here to stay, and that the
responsibility of endowment-fund managers and the investment and financial committees of education have been
clearly defined.

These institutions must, in the final analysis,
recognize that there is no such thing as being neutral
on these issues. Whatever you do, you are in some sense
taking sides. The search is for a better flow of information and theses for making thoughtful decisions.

PROCESS: INCORPORATION OF SOCIAL CONCERNS INTO CORPORATE PROCESS

What is the proper mechanism for addressing social
concerns within the corporate structure? How might issues of corporate social responsibility be included in
the managerial agenda with the greatest effectiveness?
Is adversary or advisory lobbying more effective in pre-
senting social interest concerns to corporation management? The contours of these questions are sharpened when
a specific model is proposed as the best process for in-
corporating social concerns into corporate practice.

The issue emerged as an important conference theme
because Roger F. Murray's discussion of the role of the
professional institutional investor in the context of increasing demands and challenges from other socially active stockholders raised them. He found that the issue
of stockholder responsibility drove him to stress the
need for "a structure for orderly and informed dealing
with newly emerging issues of direct relevance to all
participants in the corporate enterprise," and proposes
the mechanism of a corporate "advisory panel" to deal
with the need. An abridged version of his paper constitutes Chapter 5.

Chapter 6 includes comments on Dr. Murray's advisory
panel suggestion, as well as other suggestions on how social issues might enter the corporation. The question,
"Who should influence decisions of societal concern?" is
also raised, not so much as a threat to the role of management in making such decisions, but as a concern that
various elements of society be heard.

Mr. E. M. Estes, Executive Vice President of General
Motors Corporation, discusses the function of the General
Motors Public Policy Committee in Chapter 7. Though General Motors management is apparently well satisfied with
the role the public policy committee plays in bringing
social concerns into the corporation, some consultation
participants expressed less enthusiasm. The primary
criticism of the General Motors process is that the committee's reports and findings are not made available for
public scrutiny.

A discussion among members of a special consultation
committee assigned the task of examining how social concerns might be structured into the corporation is found

in Chapter 8. The committee reached general consensus on
the need for an internal mechanism to oversee corporate
responsibility issues, but opinions varied on the specific
makeup, function, and decision-making power of such a
mechanism. Most participants agreed that information
gathering, policy formulation, performance auditing, and
policy implementation should be functions of any mechanism charged with monitoring corporate social responsibility. Yet some participants expressed doubt that such
mechanisms within corporations would alone be enough to
assure societal satisfaction in areas of conflict. Governmental action was suggested by some of these persons;
others advocated the continuance of more informal and
varied pressure.

5

THE INSTITUTIONAL STOCKHOLDER AS INVESTOR AND OWNER
Roger F. Murray

The purpose of this paper is to examine the potential role of institutional investors in the processes by which the modern corporation deals with the full range of social and ethical, as well as business and financial, problems which face it in the 1970s. The title seeks to recognize the real world, not the fictional environment in which investment is treated as separate and distinct from ownership.

Given the inevitability of institutional involvement in corporate affairs and decisions, an effort is made to deal with social responsibility issues in this context, seeking to develop a viable and consistent behavior pattern for influential stockholders. Here the most complicated and controversial issues must be addressed and the conflicts recognized. This writer's conclusions--and they are only one man's opinions--are presented for examination and discussion, not as definite answers, but as possible stimuli to the search for more rational, thoughtful, and consistent responses from the American business system to the insistent questions being raised by a volatile, socially conscious society of the affluent 1970s.

Dr. Murray is the S. Sloan Colt Professor of Banking and Finance, Graduate School of Business, Columbia University. A lifelong investment manager, he is currently serving as a trustee or director of such institutional investors as mutual funds, educational endowments, property and life insurance companies, a mutual savings bank, and other institutions.

THE INVESTOR ROLE OF THE INSTITUTION

Unlike the individual, who is perfectly free to do whatever he chooses with his investment portfolio, the institutional investor is accountable and responsible to stockholders, policyholders, beneficiaries, participants, donors, and other interested parties. There is a presumption that, within the range of risk-taking appropriate to the specific circumstances, the institution has the single objective of maximizing the productivity of the assets across a span of time of medium to long duration.

Over the years the proportion of voting securities held by institutions has increased. In addition the management of portfolios has become substantially better paid, highly competitive, and closely watched. In this environment the natural accommodation is for the portfolio manager to concentrate on his problems of selection and timing and to leave all decisions about the portfolio company's affairs to corporate management. "If you don't like the management, sell the stock" is the familiar expression of this attitude. The institutional investor has been happy to be the "silent partner" of corporate management.[1] Individual stockholders have been in no position to evaluate or to challenge the conduct of corporate management in complicated business decisions.[2]

In summary, the trend of events has reinforced the position of self-perpetuating corporate managements responsible in the short run only to boards of directors of their own choosing. The discipline of the market for equity securities operates, of course, over the longer run to determine the cost and availability of capital to managements, but we all know how slowly this can operate and for what long periods publicly owned businesses can be operated with no apparent responsibility of managements to anyone but themselves.

THE OWNERSHIP ROLE OF THE INSTITUTION

Fortunately the existing structure works quite well in sustaining the drive for the efficiency and productivity of the system. The threat of the stock market's discipline is usually present to reinforce the manager's own sense of pride and motivation to be effectively competitive. Financial incentives are supplemented by a wide variety of nonmonetary rewards for success.

It works well, therefore, to leave all day-to-day operating business decisions to incumbent managements. Only at major points of decision (such as mergers and acquisitions, major financing, and the determination of important lines of business) is the institutional investor tempted to speak his piece as a part-owner of the business.

In the rare cases in which a major corporate decision is involved, the reluctant institution may be forced into its role as an owner as a last resort when all other courses of action, especially sale of the stock, have been found undesirable or ineffective. Acting like an owner is seldom a satisfactory alternative, because a well-entrenched management with the proxy machinery firmly in its hands will brush off most representations even by important institutional stockholders.[3] Corporate management knows full well that institutions dread being held up as "concentrations of economic power" if the exercise of their rights of ownership occurs in public view. Any collaboration among institutions is, of course, even more subject to challenge.

Thus, acting like an owner is an unfamiliar role for the institutional investor in public-held corporations. He is ill at ease and readily made to feel like a crank if he ventures to question the continued transfer of authority and responsibility to incumbent managements. Corporate public relations and stockholder relations efforts, aided by able legal and financial counselors, are well equipped to smother any but the most vigorously raised voice of dissent.

NEW AND UNUSUAL CHALLENGES

In this environment it is difficult enough for the informed and conscientious institutional investor to challenge a portfolio company's management on a conventional matter of business or financial policy. To raise questions about the employment of women and minorities, ecological safeguards, product quality, overseas operations, health and safety standards, and community involvement requires venturing into entirely new and uncharted seas. With no established norms, no readily applicable analytical framework, no visible addition to the "bottom line" for socially responsible behavior, and no appropriate forum for discussion, the reaction of corporate managements has been extraordinarily defensive and even peevish.

Highly placed executives have demonstrated an extreme sensitivity to even the mildest questioning of their omniscience in dealing with social and ethical issues.

The knowledgeable, temperate institutional investors did not raise questions about these new dimensions of corporate activities. The silent partners were almost as silent as ever.

In the absence of calm, deliberate, and judicious discussion of the need for adaptation and change, not to new markets or new technologies but to new and unusual public expectations, the field was left to bright, articulate, and often abrasive activists from outside the Establishment. As corporate managements overreacted to what they considered unfair baiting and overstatement of the issues, it became almost impossible for the thoughtful institutional investor to find his place at a confrontation between crusading inexperience and obdurate insensitivity. There was no middle ground to be found between the extreme views of the protagonists.

Now the institutional investor, in many cases admitting past failures to perceive the seriousness of the emerging corporate responsibility issues, is seeking to find his proper role as investor-owner. Enlightened corporate managements have relaxed and undertaken thoughtful analysis and discussion of the complicated situations they face. Voluntary groups continue to function effectively as catalysts and investigators of hitherto secret crannies of private and public institutional structures. At this writing, this first phase has been completed. The awakening, the confrontations, the legal maneuvering, the charge and countercharge, and the limited involvement of the reluctant institutional investor have all taken place. The results have been rather spectacular in many respects, but major issues have still to be resolved when they arise outside of the traditional business and financial spheres.

The complexities of the profit-and-loss system in allocating resources in our economy are enough to engage the best minds of each generation. Now we are adding another dimension in the form of responsibilities of business organizations to contribute to, or at least not to detract from, a standard of living that emphasizes the quality of life as well as the quantity of material goods and services. A few moments of reflection will suffice to destroy the illusion of easy solutions to the problems being raised by this new dimension.

There is no evidence that disregard for social and ethical standards of conduct is consistently more profitable than seeking to observe them. Indeed the evidence appears to argue that, on the contrary, it is responsible behavior that leads to broad public acceptance of the service or product offered for sale. But this does not mean that costs generated by environmental protection, product safety, special training programs, and similar projects can be internalized by a single firm attempting to be a leader in its industry. The economic pressure is to be about average in response, to take steps only as required by law or the administrative actions of government. But the institutions, as large holders of major public corporations, may be pressured to seek leadership rather than mere compliance from their portfolio companies.

The economics of socially responsible behavior are highly uncertain in any particular situation at any one point in time. If institutional investors, as owners, decide to exert their influence on portfolio companies to undertake leadership roles with highly uncertain consequences for profitability, corporate managements are entitled to ask such questions as the following:

1. By what process was it determined that this particular responsibility to society outweighs other traditional and more clearly defined obligations to the firm's several publics?

2. Does the investing institution purport to speak for all institutions? for a majority of stockholders? How does one measure the breadth of participation in a particular line of thought?

3. Who is the arbiter of responsible conduct in complicated situations in which even the full range of facts may not be agreed upon?

4. How can decisions affecting corporate actions in social matters be separated from the stream of managerial decisions on strictly business questions?

These and similar questions are enough to make a busy executive react with a feeling that he only wants these new challenges to go away and to leave him with the more than adequate challenge presented by the conventional profit-and-loss statement.

STRICTURES AND STRUCTURES

Ethically motivated expositions of points of view and expressions of opinion about corporate conduct are all too frequently greeted as the ill-considered and impractical prattling of minds too little occupied with the realities of meeting a payroll in a competitive environment. The reactions of corporate managements are all too frequently characterized as excessively defensive presentations, freighted with legalistic and public relations clichés which are not responsive to the basic issues. If the controversial matter is tortured into the format of a proxy statement, the chances of developing rational discussions are even further reduced. These methods of frustrating communication are more apt to give rise to mutual recriminations than to serious exploration of the issues.

The critical factors seem to be an apparent challenge to the corporate manager's decision-making prerogatives and the implied accusation that his lack of social sensitivity and ethical awareness disqualifies him as a judge of responsible action. The reality, of course, is that neither party is the sole repository of wisdom in such complicated matters.

A promising solution might be to introduce a third party to the situation. An advisory panel of perhaps three or five individuals could be recruited by that committee of the board of directors which would be specifically charged with dealing with public interest questions. The corporation would compensate and provide staff support to this panel, but its independence would have to be assured in order to make its work effective and its voice influential in resolving controversies.

The panel would receive all communications from stockholders, voluntary associations, and public officials for evaluation and recommendations. The distinctive feature of their consultative and advisory roles would be the publication of their conclusions in employee magazines, reports to stockholders, or special releases. While the opinions would be purely advisory, they would carry considerable weight when reached after careful study of the facts and patient hearing of all points of view. It would be possible, of course, for a knowledgeable panel to report on the complexities of a particular subject without reaching specific conclusions at a certain point in time.

Most important would be the advisory panel's exploration and presentation of topics that have not yet entered the arena of heated argument. By commissioning research projects on their own initiative, the panel would seek to anticipate and not simply to respond to the currents of change in our industrial society. Reports from the panel could be presented at the annual meeting and members would be present to listen and respond to stockholder questions.

Some will argue that the advisory panel will tend to take decisions away from those responsible for managing the enterprise. Others will contend that the panel will have no real influence on the course of events, since they are beholden to the corporate executives for their positions. The remedy for such extreme conclusions is found in the continuous publicizing of findings of fact and recommendations for action, as well as the qualifications of the panel members. Independence of thought and action should be adequately protected and its absence conspicuously evident.

Returning to the four questions previously identified as being appropriately raised by managers, the advisory panel would help to develop the process for determining social priorities and offer a judgment, not a decision, as to the appropriate course of action. The institutional investor, alone or in concert with others, would be assured of a thoughtful hearing, and the panel could determine whether a particular point of view is widely shared.

In the finding of facts, the hearing of arguments, and the expression of conclusions, the advisory panel would be serving in the pattern of the commission often appointed outside of the regular structure of government to provide fresh perspectives and insights on old problems. The appointing authority is not bound by the commission's report; yet its recommendations, if well thought out, have frequently proved influential in future decisions and programs.

Compared with alternatives such as the appointment of "public interest" corporate directors on presently constituted boards or the recruiting of ad hoc panels to deal with single issues, the permanent advisory panel has much to recommend it.[4] It is not a lightning rod, nor is it the keeper of the corporate conscience, but it can provide a structure for orderly and informed dealing with newly emerging issues of direct relevance to all participants in the corporate enterprise.

The possible improvement of corporate relationships with institutional investor-owners could be dramatic. The present frictions and frustrations could be replaced by serious and deliberate discussions. The serious stockholder would be free to raise whatever issues seemed to be important to his constituencies in an atmosphere free of rigid adherence to protocol.

CONCLUDING OBSERVATIONS

The preceding ideas for creating a new structure for
the ventilation and resolution of issues in new and unfamiliar areas of corporate responsibility are unlikely to
win unanimous support. The objective, however, must be
served in some constructive way. Investing institutions
must respond to their constituents' preferences and must
find a way to reflect them in forms of activity other than
the purchase and sale of shares.

The commitment of institutions to the long-term via-
bility and productivity of the business system is repre-
sented by very large (about $300 billion) investments in
corporate equity securities. The acceptance, or prefer-
ably the approbation, by our society of the manner in
which large publicly owned corporate enterprises conduct
their affairs is critical to the institutions' ability to
discharge their functions effectively and to enjoy future
growth. The institutions cannot be indifferent to any
dimension of the manner in which corporate managements
deal with their publics.

Finally, it is essential that the achievement of constructive change and the adaptation of corporate attitudes
be a joint venture rather than an adversary proceeding.
Corporate managements need to be supported, cajoled,
prodded, and encouraged more than they need to be attacked,
confronted, ridiculed, and written off as hopeless. The
institutions, with their tremendous commitment to the productivity of equity investment, really have no alternative
but to press for a more rational, effective, and timely
response from corporate managements to the demands of a
critical, impatient social order.

NOTES

1. This term was given content in Daniel J. Baum and
Ned B. Stiles, The Silent Partners: Institutional Investors and Corporate Control (Syracuse, N.Y.: Syracuse University Press, 1965).

2. The drive for "shareholder democracy" contributed
by Lewis Gilbert et al. has dealt mainly with simple and
straightforward issues which can be presented as black or
white. Complicated business problems, not to mention

social responsibility issues, are eschewed by these self-appointed representatives of the individual stockholder.

3. Institutional Relationships with Portfolio Companies, Institutional Investor Study Report of the Securities and Exchange Commission, 5 (Washington: U.S. Government Printing Office, 1971). Similar findings came from the SEC's 1966 report, Public Policy Implications of Investment Company Growth.

4. A five-member panel might have single five-year terms for its members to assure a fresh flow of ideas along with the continuity necessary for well-informed conclusions. Outside directors would not be ineligible to serve.

COMMENTS ON THE "CORPORATE
ADVISORY PANEL" PROPOSAL

<u>James Lee</u>: I have given considerable thought to Dr.
Murray's suggestion and believe the advisory panel is a
good idea in theory, but perhaps a difficult one to implement with effectiveness. It certainly could provide several minds devoting their full time to issues of social
responsibility, assisting a busy management saddled with
many other problems as well. Yet if a management is inclined to turn a deaf ear or be insensitive to public pressures for positive action, even such a panel could be out-
maneuvered or ignored.

Choosing the members of the panel would be difficult
in the first place. I also doubt that any management--
good, bad, or indifferent--would be willing to agree to
publication of the panel's conclusions if the management
was in disagreement with those conclusions.

Finally, Dr. Murray states that investing institutions
must respond to their constituencies' preferences and must
find a way to reflect them in forms of activity other than
the purchase and sale of shares. I would like to know just
how the constituents' preferences are determined with ownership as fragmented as it is. How is the management of an
institution or a fund going to determine what his constituency's preferences are?

<u>Robert Potter</u>: We are talking about willingness to have
committees and that it should be constructive and that
there should not be confrontation. Then why don't corporations have some of these interests on their boards of
directors? What is the resistance to having on the board
as many responsible people as possible who are not out to
wreck the corporation? Why has there been this resistance?

Terrance Hanold: The problem, I suppose, is that the private corporate world has been very private for a hundred years. Now the public corporation is really more public than almost any institution in society today, including all of the churches, so far as its exposure to influence, its receptivity to ideas, and its willingness to accept and to implement. The fact that historically the level of contact was small has meant that there has been no habit of turning to a variety of people for membership on the board. In addition, our circle of contacts is not wide enough, and we simply do not know enough people to approach.

Mr. Potter: Generally speaking, you agree that the psychology of management, both management internally and the board, is against having second guessers? It is just too difficult to cope with in your day-to-day operations?

Mr. Hanold: No. That, of course, is the point about the board. They don't get into your day-to-day operations. Managers are the people who are there day-to-day, who can affect what can be done, and who, of course, work within the general policies laid down by the board. But the board does not get into day-to-day management.

Mr. Potter: The point I am trying to make is that if you had someone of the type I suggested on your board you would have a concern that he would try to get into day-to-day management.

Mr. Hanold: No, for the reason, I think, that a board member can influence management's point of view. But it is pretty difficult for them to take the responsibility or attempt to take the responsibility for precise acts within the business or the firm. They will not do it. They cannot do it. Management really cannot let them do it, because it is an abdication of responsibility that is placed on management and that management must answer for.

SOCIAL ISSUES AND CORPORATE DECISION-MAKING

Timothy Smith: In the present management model, how do we introduce social challenge and change? Where are the issues going to come from that the management model will deal with? I think that what we are talking about here is ways in which corporations can know about certain complex situations. I do not see how the complex situations are going to be faced, even with Roger Murray's model, which takes away doubts and conflicts of interest. I am not convinced that from his model the board will pick up a new source of corporate responsibility. It is going to be people who have outside viewpoints and who are immersed in a concern who are going to bring an issue to the corporation as a pressure group. It is going to be the people who are directly related to an issue. It is going to be black people who are directing issues most critically with regard to minority hiring.

Mr. Potter: The committee approach that Dr. Murray suggests concerns me. I feel it puts the problem once removed from where the actors are. I have something I would like to lay on the table as an alternative.

The board of directors as we know it today has considerable power. It selects management, management selects it, and so on. I feel that the board should be pinned with social responsibility and that the board should be "greened" to the extent that it incorporates the committee that Dr. Murray is suggesting. It should be incorporated as a direct line operation in the sense that it should deal with affirmative social action programs as part of a total corporate social responsibility program. I think to deal other than holistically with these issues will limit the confrontation of social responsibility issues to a small area within the corporation.

In my experience in the last two or three years in this area, corporations do not want to deal with the broad social issues in the country. They are very defensive about them. Some corporations admit to being defensive about such issues because they don't know how to handle them. Therefore they like to set up committees and study groups. Many corporations have done so.

Yet I haven't seen to date any published reports or results of actions of these committees or study groups. I think they are sponges. The burden is on the corporate community, if the committee route is to be followed, to show that it is not just another sponge to absorb the so-called corporate responsibility movement in this country. In sum, I am still old-fashioned enough to hope that the individual on the board and in management will act with a social conscience, because the only alternative that I can see will be government control of the corporate structures.

Roger Murray: I think you are talking about where our society looks for the solution of problems. I believe

that with many problems decentralization of decision-making
is desirable, efficient, and highly productive. This means
that in many cases in our diverse society we should prefer
the allocation of decision-making processes to individual
firms in individual situations operating under a variety
of restraints rather than to substitute a centralized planning agency of government.

In my advocacy of additional structures within the
corporation I would hope to improve the quality of corporate responsiveness in solving problems. My basic conviction is that a more responsive, alert, imaginative, and
innovative business structure will produce better results
than the long delayed and sometimes blundering response of
government in dealing with some of these very complicated
questions. I think we have evidence that government really
has found it very difficult to respond to such a wide range
of complicated, intricate issues in a way that is satisfactory to our society. This should encourage us to seek better, more decentralized, and potentially more responsive
ways of problem solving through the private business structure, if we can indeed gear up that structure to perform
effectively and responsibly.

WHO SHOULD INFLUENCE CORPORATE DECISIONS
ON SOCIAL RESPONSIBILITY?

Byron Grant: The question remains: Who is going to make
the decisions? You can put in a committee to try to make
decisions. Yet who is to say that a group or a commission
that you select is going to act or behave one iota differ-
ently when confronted with the same kinds of problems that
management is currently facing? Nothing is going to eliminate somebody somewhere from criticizing or thinking that
they are not doing things correctly. If you take decision-
making away from the freedom of the individual, whether it
is corporate management or whatever group that you put in,
you move in an altogether different direction. At that
point you are moving toward a community thing. If you
move far enough into the community thing, you move into a
state thing.

Lincoln Eldredge: That is not what I hear being discussed.
I don't think anybody here is suggesting that the final
authority of decision-making be taken out of management's
hands.

What I hear being talked about in terms of Dr.
Murray's panel is an advisory committee that carries more

clout than the PTA. It is supposedly made up of reputable, thinking, intelligent, sincere people who perhaps bring a different perspective to a management decision. They offer their suggestions, but the final authority rests with management and management alone. I think that the setting up of a dichotomy between free enterprise and state control or socialism is incorrect.

Mr. Potter: I think one of the reasons corporate responsibility groups have opted for pressuring business rather than government is the feeling that business is the acting process in the national picture in many areas. For instance, I think it would be arguable that United States foreign policy vis-à-vis South Africa is the $100 billion that is invested in South Africa by American corporations as opposed to what the President might say in the White House.

Business influence in Washington on executive and legislative levels is another area. An example of this would be in the Rhodesian chrome issue, where one company was able to lobby Congress and have the embargo lifted for chrome.

How does the community affect, or try at least to exercise, some balance of influence when a corporation has the power to lobby? There are two ways. One way is to lobby in government itself, if the corporation has the power and resources to lobby Congress. The second way is to lobby the corporation.

7

GENERAL MOTORS' PUBLIC POLICY COMMITTEE

FUNCTION OF THE PUBLIC POLICY COMMITTEE

E. M. Estes: We are very pleased with the function of our public policy committee at General Motors. They have certainly asked us a great many questions about our business. I think it is serving a good audit kind of function on our operations and on our management.

We have a bonus and salary committee on the Board of Directors made up entirely of outside directors. We have an audit committee also made up entirely of outside directors. Now we have a public policy committee similarly constituted. We have been very pleased with the way that they have taken up problems and brought them to our attention. Periodically, we have been asked for a management point of view to report to the public policy committee.

Lincoln Eldredge: In what way has this committee helped your company in terms of profit or general good will or any other standard you want to use?

Mr. Estes: It is pretty hard to put dollar signs on good will and corporate responsibility and other things we are concerned about. I wouldn't know how to do that. I believe the public policy committee is at least attempting to serve the function that is being discussed here--that is, to have an outside look at management and see whether we are progressive enough and whether we are moving fast enough and whether we are taking on the kinds of problems that we should.

Robert Potter: What is the makeup of the policy committee? Is it predominantly management, outside management, presidents of other companies?

Robert T. O'Connell: There are nonemployee directors.
They are the Chairman of Mellon Bank in Pittsburgh, the
Chairman of Allied Chemical, the Honorary Chairman of MIT,
a retired Vice Chairman of GM, and the President of Mar-
shall Field in Chicago.

Mr. Potter: They are pretty much people who are similarly situated to your own management in the sense that they
have similar problems. In other words, the committee is
not green.

Mr. Estes: In selecting a committee, the objective was
to get a cross-section of backgrounds and views.

Mr. O'Connell: The public policy committee was established in August 1970. At that time the board had evaluated various information flow alternatives to assure responsiveness to current trends. The board ultimately
felt that a committee of the full board, which has the
knowledge of and responsibility for running the business,
but is independent to the degree of not being employees
of General Motors, was the best way to go.
    When the public policy committee started looking at
the public aspects of the corporation's operations, they
basically had to evaluate the most effective way to assure an accurate and balanced evaluation. The members
brought different skills to the committee themselves. In
the technological area, they saw that to do the job that
was necessary required the concentrated efforts of a committee of technical experts, which was subsequently established. In several other areas, they felt that they could
get sufficient input from one or two meetings with specific experts.
    The chairman of the board generally attends a portion
of each meeting, so the committee has the opportunity at
least once a month of having the chairman sit down and
listen to what is on their minds. The committee reviews
all areas of the business as they relate to public policy
and then makes recommendations to the board of directors
or to management.

Stephen Farber: Does the committee report at all to the
public or beyond?

Mr. O'Connell: The committee reports periodically to the
board, as all standing committees do, on all their actions.
Right now it is on about a six-month cycle.

PUBLIC DISCLOSURE--AN ISSUE OF CREDIBILITY

<u>Dr. Farber</u>: But they don't report publicly? There is no
public report? Is that contemplated? As things stand,
it is sort of a mystery wrapped in an enigma. I can understand that it may be very helpful to the corporation
internally, and from what you say obviously some crucial
issues have been brought up which are apparently being
considered very seriously. But it is sort of hard to
know that for sure. There are people outside the corporation who might have some interest in it. What is your
feeling on that?

<u>Mr. O'Connell</u>: Well, first of all, as to disclosure of
how the public policy committee operates and generally
what it does, we have been having institutional investor
conferences now for the last couple of years and have
been distributing copies of various presentations to our
stockholders and other thought leaders. These presentations have given some information on the public policy
committee and selected recommendations.
     As far as a detailed, comprehensive disclosure of
the specific recommendations made by the public policy
committee, it is not believed to be in the best interest
of the corporation or its stockholders that a detailed
listing of every area of examination or recommendation be
published. In relying on outside consultants as well as
GM management, a more frank and responsive discussion is
achieved by not having each incidental thing subject to a
public disclosure. The final policy judgment of the corporation exists at the full board of directors level.
The point is that the public policy committee is kind of
a crystallizing agent. The committee points out areas of
public policy concern and discusses alternative correc-
tive approaches with management. The committee then says,
"Talk with us again in the future and let us see how you
have done in terms of how we interpret these public issues as they relate to General Motors."

<u>Dr. Farber</u>: Wasn't it your point, Dr. Murray, that such
a committee should make a public report, or am I mistaken?

<u>Dr. Murray</u>: You are quite correct. My thought was that
obviously they were not required to report the minutes of
every meeting and obviously they were not required to report prematurely on their deliberations, but whenever
their thinking is crystallized, one of the very important

provisions of my proposal was that they had the privilege or the option at their own discretion to publish the results of their recommendation. Corporate management could of course respond or answer or object or anything else, but the key factor involved in assuring the independence of this kind of activity was their right to make their deliberations public.

Another aspect of the same thing, it seems to me, is the whole question of credibility. Clearly one of the problems of the present committee structure is that a great many people are going to raise questions of credibility. As long as this is kept in this particular style, it seems to me that a large part of General Motors' public is never really going to be satisfied, no matter how well the company committee is in fact functioning. They still will not be prepared to believe this until the company as a matter of policy would want to gain the acceptance of their effort and undertaking by giving this kind of action publicity.

Mr. Estes: We would hope that the public policy committee is going to do enough for our management so that the conduct of the corporation shows an improvement in these areas. I think what we are trying to do is have our public posture be such that we will be less criticized in the future.

Dr. Murray: That is a very commendable point of view. I think I understand it. I am thoroughly sympathetic. The question I would raise, of course, is whether this is really adequately responsive to an impatient public that is looking at our large public corporations and asking a great deal, at times asking totally unreasonable things of corporate management in our present society.

The question is: How effectively are you responding? Are there ways in which, for example, you would show that you were so relaxed about the operations of your public policy committee and so confident in the responsiveness of your management that you couldn't care less if they published every part of their deliberations? This would have a smashing impact on public opinion of General Motors. I say without fear of contradiction that that kind of openness is what a great many people are looking for and are not finding.

Mr. Estes: Isn't this the function/mechanism argument coming back? That is really what we are talking about

about now. Do you want a report on the mechanism or do you want a report on the function?

Kirk O. Hanson: In the series of demands that the public is making on corporations for certain types of social action, for certain types of solutions for social problems, there are a couple of demands that relate directly to the questions of disclosure and the actual mechanism whereby the corporation is making other social decisions. I think there are two demands. Number one, for openness and disclosure. Number two, for some kind of participatory mechanism. Those can be stated as separate demands upon the corporation, two demands that relate to specific impact on social questions.

I think that the reason that people would say General Motors should have a policy of disclosure concerning the public policy committee is that they have seen issues become important in and of themselves, such as the openness of the whole process, the openness of information, and what is going on within the firm.

STRUCTURING SOCIAL CONCERNS
INTO THE CORPORATE
DECISION-MAKING PROCESS

<u>Howard Chase</u>: Our committee was given the task of ponder-
ing the question, "How might social concerns be structured
into the decision-making process of a corporation?" Con-
comitant to this question we found the following questions: "Where in the corporation does this information
come in? Where in the corporation is there most likely
to be an adequate sensing mechanism or device with the
priorities established on what the corporation intends to
do? Then, where does the action take place?"
     In an attempt to achieve some structure we should
discuss first internal and then external procedures for
filtering social concerns and structuring social concerns
into the corporation.
     The internal requisites for a device to structure so-
cial concerns into the decision-making process of a corporation follow somewhat in this order of priority. There
must first be a firm intellectual and emotional commitment for the filtering of concerns from the chief executive officer. Secondly, the chief executive officer must
have a system or process of structuring the concerns.
Thirdly, problems should be dispersed as quickly as possible into the operating divisions of the corporation, or
into the profit centers of the corporation. The division

     Early in the consultation the chairman, Charles M.
Judd, appointed a committee of participants to give some
concentrated attention to the subject stated above by the
committee chairman. The discussion in this brief section
is a sample of the dialogue among the group following the
chairman's report.

or profit center heads must get into the act to establish some kind of consensus. The point is to broaden the arena of the discussion of social concerns.

Finally, the structuring of social concerns into the decision-making process must in some way be evaluated in an annual performance review. Just as the manager's contribution toward the profit and well-being of the corporation is annually considered in performance reviews, so also must management's social performance be evaluated. Some of this evaluation can be quantified. For example, quantified results of minority employment are possible.

We generally agreed that the internal structure of evaluation should be an internal committee on corporate responsibility. Conceivably it could be made up of the vice presidents of various operating divisions, or might be composed of the people selected by the separate profit centers to conduct their own analysis or examination of how this process is to take place.

We move now to the second area, the external requisites to the successful defining of an answer to the question that has been raised, "What are the sensing or policy-influencing mechanisms that can be applied from the outside?"

The committee has suggested a variety of models. There has been the General Motors model, the conventional boardroom, the general legislative approach to force structuring of social concerns in the corporation decision-making, the use of a shareholders' responsibility committee, and so on.

There was a good deal of discussion on endorsement of some kind of a public policy committee as the best sensing device for filtering social concerns into the corporation decision-making process, some device that would provide some catalytic agent where the internal results, or the internal systems that were used, whatever they are, and the external forces could meet to find the correct questions for translation into corporate policy. The questions arose immediately as to who is to appoint such a body, who supports it, and what will happen to its recommendations.

Richard B. Smith: I would like to deal with the corporate organization model as it exists today. The shareholders elect a board of directors. The directors hold office only by reason of their election by the shareholders. The board of directors elects the officers of the company, the chief executive officer, and his top executive managers.

71

I believe most people recognize that the board of
directors in large, publicly owned companies is nominated
and selected by the management, which controls the proxy
machinery. This usually results in the election of the
nominees who are selected. There are large variations on
that in corporate practice--for instance, where a take-
over, merger, or proxy contest occurs--and smaller varia-
tions--for instance, where a committee of outside directors does the nominating. Thus, there are ways in which
the ultimate legal power of the shareholders to replace
the board is exercised. Every board and every management
recognizes that this can be exercised in any company at
some point. Nevertheless, while the legal model is that
the shareholders control the board and that the board ap-
points the management, in practice the flow of control is
a lot more complicated than that, and in most large companies it is the executive management group that in effect nominates and selects the board.

The important thing is, it works. At least it did
work until some people began to feel that the modern corporation was not being responsive to the external "publics" with which it dealt--consumers, neighbors, the environment, the government; that it was not as responsive
as it should be to the growing interest in considerations
beyond the management of physical and human assets of the
company for a narrowly defined profit objective.

Today the corporation is called upon to direct itself toward such crucial matters as minority economic
conditions, environmental pollution, and broadened concepts of community safety. Yet the corporate structure
was not being very responsive to those expressed concerns;
indeed it showed something of a disinclination to try to
manage such problems that lay beyond the traditional business area.

I think most corporations today realize these are
problems. In order for the corporation to exist today,
its management must somehow at least address such problems. The question is, how do you institutionalize social responsibility within a corporate legal model that
itself does not always reflect the actual state of affairs but nevertheless has worked.

One suggestion is that you have a public policy committee composed of people independent and separate from
the management and the board. Such a committee would prepare reports that would be made public, go to the shareholders, the press, and everybody else, and would be a
separate center for the formulation of public policies.

One of the complexities of a separate group able to look into corporate matters and make public reports is the enormously difficult problem of what is, or should be, competitively protected information. (I don't think that there is any company in its right mind that would elect such a committee.)

There is another model that several companies now have, quite close to what General Motors now has in response to such pressures as have been described. It is a standing committee of the board, a "public policy" committee that is a subunit of the board. It would have some sort of staff of its own, employed by the corporation.

A third model is to have as part of the executive management a specially designated senior officer, vice president or above in status, as a kind of public affairs officer. His functions would be about the same as the directors' committee but he would be an officer selected by the management (and elected by the board of directors) totally integrated within the executive management.

Whatever mechanism is employed within the corporate structure, I believe we have identified four functions to be performed: information gathering, policy formulation, performance auditing, and policy implementation. First, information must be collected from as many sources, inside and outside the company, as possible. The point is that the normal corporate information gathering system has not been attuned to the kind of information we are talking about here. The second function would be formulation of policy: Based upon the information gathered, what are the community and corporate needs? The third function, auditing performance, would go beyond gathering information, and would gauge the way in which the corporation is in fact performing in these areas. Trying to develop criteria by which you can judge whether the corporation is performing satisfactorily would be part of this task. The last function regards implementing whatever public policy conclusions the corporation adopts, and making sure that they are in fact implemented.

I think it is implicit that any mechanism would have to have some kind of a staff of its own. In some cases they would have to employ consultants, have an outsider prepare a report, come in and look at a particular matter with fresh eyes, new ideas, and new approaches. It is very easy, of course, to look at things from the outside without adequate information about the real problems the management has to deal with.

A committee of directors would have, it seems to me, a better relationship with the executive management of the company in terms of getting access to information and having an impact on policy formulation and evaluating results. Implementation, of course, is clearly a management function.

Robert James: We may want to recognize that a committee of the board at this time may be appropriate, but in time we may want to see more than one committee. It is possible that in some boards organized today you will already find the kinds of things we are talking about that fall into the province of some of these committees. Consequently, I am much more concerned with trying to get information to the kinds of people who would use it effectively, and allowing much of the concern for organization to be a developing thing, a naturally growing thing meeting the needs of corporations and society. My real concern is that we find a way of making some parts of what goes on in the corporation today public, getting some of the information out in verifiable form on a consistent reporting basis.

Anthony Connole: My idea is somewhat at variance with everything that has been discussed thus far. It is based upon an assumption of some level of current dissatisfaction with the social performance of the corporation and the further assumption that the public allegations of social responsibility by corporations are not going to stand the tide of public demand for greater social accountability.

I have great doubts about the ability of any kind of in-house structure, particularly any single in-house structure, to achieve the desired results. I would like to see a dual system. One would be a voluntary system, and the backup to it would be legislative input. I think that this is necessary, so that when the voluntary system fails, the legislative input would be there to assure social progress by the corporation.

I feel the legislative backup is an absolute necessity. I have my doubts about the ability of management, even with outside stimulation, to really make the somewhat difficult decisions, largely by reason of competition. If there is one company that steps out ahead of its competitors, it suffers in the stock market. It could also suffer in terms of cost of producing the product or the service, unless its competitors join it. The only

feasible way to get a whole industry to move forward together in cost and social areas is by legislation.

<u>Charles Powers</u>: I sense among all of us a recognition
that the corporation is a very anomalous institution.
The legal structure that was originally set up for corporations is appropriate to voluntary associations, that
is, associations in which the people who participate or
are affected do so voluntarily. Most modern corporations
are no longer voluntary associations in the traditional
sense.

   Modern corporations have taken on public functions,
and every one of us realizes that somehow we have to figure out what to do with this institution which, though
previously thought of solely in terms of economics and
production, now has to take on, because of its public
role, new kinds of responsibilities and forms.

   We are not going to come up with a single model that
handles all of the questions, precisely because the corporation is an anomalous institution and because corporations differ so dramatically in size and types of societal
impact. It is when we become sophisticated enough to see
that the simple "public-private" dichotomy we impose on a
complex and highly differentiated economic system isn't
adequate that we will be ready to see which of the several
mechanisms we have discussed--and some we do not yet have
imagination to see--are appropriate to specific corporate
contexts.

PART

IV

PRACTICE: A CASE STUDY
OF GENERAL MOTORS
SOUTH AFRICAN

In recent years the criticism of American corporations that have operations in southern Africa has grown. Investors, most noticeably churches, have focused their attention on what the American corporation's impact is in South Africa and what such corporations might do to further racial and social justice in that country.

Perhaps in response to these pressures, General Motors has brought about a number of changes in areas of employment, job training, and education, giving more African and Colored South Africans a variety of new employment opportunities. The general belief held by General Motors, as well as by other foreign corporations with plants and operations in South Africa, is that the presence of U.S. companies in that country represents an "important force toward progressive change." This is the well-publicized rationale which General Motors offers in response to those who criticize its continued operation in South Africa. Not only are its employment practices aimed at upgrading the economic status of its African and Colored employees, General Motors suggests, but the company hopes others will follow its example.

A report of General Motors' changes in operating policies in its South African subsidiary, presented to the consultation by Mr. E. M. Estes (Chapter 9), has been published by the corporation in pamphlet form. It is here reproduced, for it serves as a case study of a corporation's response to pressures for change in areas of societal concern and as a background for the spirited discussion it generated of issues regarding multinational corporate impact and responsibility.

Chapter 10 includes some of the discussion raised by the case study. The topics meld into each other, but at stake are such issues as the different value and political structures found abroad, the relevance and appropriateness of norms and standards to the South African situation, the validity of the thesis that economic development contributes in the long term to the undermining (or, alternatively, the maintenance) of discriminatory societal and political systems, and whether American corporations abroad shape United States foreign policy. Underlying all of these issues is the fundamental question: Can corporations facilitate real change in a society, or are they simply another element working to preserve the status quo?

Chapter 11 contains a brief dialogue on the topic of "corporate activism" and corporate responsiveness to needs in society. The dual concern for long-term planning and short-term change is brought out. The difficulty and question of desirability of corporations acting as "activists" in overseas operations is illustrated by the case of General Motors.

9

GENERAL MOTORS AND
SOUTH AFRICA
E. M. Estes

The subject of South Africa and the efforts of U.S. companies have over the past couple of years received great attention. This attention has focused on the impact of the U.S. presence on progress for the African and Colored population in that country, as well as on disclosure of information on this progress. Stockholder proposals have been submitted to numerous companies, including General Motors. The overwhelming stockholder response has provided management with a clear mandate to remain in South Africa and continue trying our best to make a positive contribution to progressive change.

General Motors has operated in South Africa for 46 years. Because we feel it to be in the best interests of our stockholders and our South African employees, we will continue to operate in South Africa.

General Motors has published a substantial amount of information on its operations in South Africa so that our stockholders, as well as the public, can make an informed judgment on this important matter. This presentation today is a manifestation of our commitment.

I will first present some background data, including important developments in 1972 and a brief description of our operations in South Africa. I will then review in

---

E. M. Estes is Executive Vice President of General Motors Corporation. He joined GM in 1934 as a cooperative student at General Motors Institute sponsored by the GM Research Laboratories and moved up to Group Vice President for Overseas Operations before being appointed to his present position in October 1972.

detail General Motors South African's ("GMSA") efforts in
various areas in which improvement is essential to the
economic and social progress of our employees. These
areas include employment and wages, training programs,
employee benefits and educational assistance, and, finally, housing assistance and recreational facilities.

DEVELOPMENTS IN 1972

The year 1972 brought some important developments.
R. C. Gerstenberg, Chairman of General Motors, visited
our South African operations in April of this year. He
returned firmly convinced that General Motors should remain in South Africa and continue its role as a leader in
upgrading the economic and social status of its employees.
The evidence was overwhelming and reflected the virtually
unanimous judgment of the many people with whom he spoke.
These included representative factory employees of GM
South African, numerous business and community leaders,
both black and white, as well as various government officials.
Additional disclosure of information on South African activities was made by several U.S. companies. As a
result, I have observed a broadening realization of the
advantages of U.S. companies remaining in South Africa as
an important force toward progressive change.
In South Africa, protests by many individuals and
groups, including blacks, churches, and students, as well
as liberal-minded whites, continued to be made against
apartheid. Further, both African leaders and church
spokesmen have become more vocal and are achieving increased visibility and identity. One leader recently
called for a single black nation in South Africa and a
land allocation more in proportion to population. He
also reportedly stated that he would not accept anything
that is short of equality. He was able to state this in
South Africa, and it was publicized in the South African
press. In addition, the first black American diplomat
was assigned to the United States Embassy in South Africa
as the Economic and Commercial Officer.
I believe these developments are all contributing to
the psychology of change in South Africa. At the same
time, more Americans have become aware of the issues involved. Overall, the year 1972 was one of advancement--
and for General Motors one of steady progress in our efforts in that country.

GENERAL MOTORS SOUTH AFRICAN

To put GM's efforts in South Africa in perspective, let me briefly describe our operating subsidiary, GM South African. GMSA's engine manufacturing plant is located at Aloes, outside of Port Elizabeth. In addition, an assembly plant and a manufacturing plant are located about ten miles away.

GM South African employs approximately 4,800 people. Over 36,000 passenger cars, commercial vehicles, and trucks were produced and sold in 1971. The subsidiary manufactures components such as engines, radiators, batteries, spark plugs, springs, and many sheet metal parts. Dollar sales totaled $140 million in 1971. Also, General Motors Acceptance Corporation conducts financing operations in South Africa through its subsidiary, GMAC South Africa (Pty.) Ltd.

General Motors' impact can be viewed in two dimensions--one, in its employment practices aimed at upgrading the economic status of its Colored and African employees, and two, as an example of progress to others.

As to the first dimension, General Motors has initiated improvement programs and is now engaged in a steady implementation phase--not cosmetic programs, but ones with direct economic benefits. Let me reassure you that General Motors plans to continue to work for social and economic progress. As a recent South African newspaper article pointed out, General Motors is viewed as a catalyst in a new phase of improvements in the working conditions of Africans and Colored in South Africa. I believe articles such as this indicate that many of the problems have been recognized and defined and the issues laid out. There is now more agreement that U.S. companies should remain in South Africa and constructively work to provide opportunities for the Africans and Colored of that country. Progress must be made in South Africa, not on a dramatic confrontation basis with its unlikely promise of success, but on a continuing day-to-day effort through progressive policies, personal contacts, and the like.

I would now like to review GM's efforts in greater detail.

GM Operating Principles

General Motors has a worldwide operating policy of equal employment opportunity. This policy has been implemented to the extent possible in each country in which we

do business. While local operating conditions may impinge
on the implementation of this policy, General Motors has
initiated affirmative action programs to upgrade its Colored and African employees in South Africa, as we have
done for black employees in the United States.

It is the established policy of GM South African
that all employees performing like work in like classification with comparable ability and seniority receive equal
pay, regardless of race. All employees have an equal opportunity for advancement at GMSA. Any employee can progress to a higher grade depending upon his ability and
performance on the job.

Extensive training programs are in operation to
broaden the impact of our equal pay policy. Further, our
benefit and educational plans are comparable to the best
provided in South African industry.

Employment

Reflecting General Motors' continuing efforts, as
well as the rapid and expanding industrialization in South
Africa, GM South African is a major employer of African
and Colored people. Colored and Africans account for 50
percent of the total work force of 4,800 employees, as
shown in Table 1.

TABLE 1

Employment

	Hourly		Salaried	Total	
	Number	Percent		Number	Percent
White	1,072	31	1,320	2,392	50
Colored	1,839	53	14	1,853	39
African	551	16	1	552	11
Total Colored and African	2,390	69	15	2,405	50
Total	3,462	100	1,335	4,797	100

These two groups comprise almost 70 percent of the
hourly work force. As to salaried employment, GMSA currently employs fourteen Colored and one African. Effective October 1, 1972, GM South African appointed its
first Colored foreman, who had previously completed his

presupervisory training in the plant. While the number of
Colored and African staff is relatively small, it is a
start--and, as such, a precedent for further progress has
been established.

GM South African hourly employment by work grade classification and race is shown in Table 2.

TABLE 2

Hourly Employment by Work Grade
Classification and Race

| Work Grade | White | Colored and African | | Total |
		Colored	African	
1	--	146	196	342
2	3	233	98	331
3	2	326	110	436
4	32	486	99	585
5	5	267	24	291
6	35	107	5	112
7	50	46	4	50
8	139	173	5	178
9	268	55	10	65
10	446	--	--	--
11	92	--	--	--
Total	1,072	1,839	551	2,390

Work grades at GM South African range from Grade 1--
the lowest classification--to Grades 10 and 11, which en-
compass highly skilled jobs to which Colored and African
employees have not yet risen.

Colored and Africans are employed mainly in the first
five grades, while most white employees are more heavily
concentrated in the upper grades. However, many Colored
employees and several Africans are in these upper grades.
Further, GM South African is conducting extensive training
programs to upgrade these race groups in the lower classifications for advancement into the more skilled Grades of
6 and above.

A measure of our employment progress is achieved by
comparing our 1972 Colored and African hourly employment
by grade with the status in early 1971, as shown in Table 3.

TABLE 3

Colored and African Hourly Employment
by Work Grade Classification

Work Grade	Oct. 1972	March 1971	1972 over or under 1971
1	342	429	-87
2	331	677	-346
3	436	597	-161
4	585	801	-216
5	291	297	-6
6	112	44	68
7	50 } 405	24 } 193	26 } 212
8	178	93	85
9	65	32	33
Total	2,390	2,994	-604

During this period, total employment for all race groups declined as a result of business conditions. Although total Colored and African employment declined by 604, it is important to note that Colored and African employees in the more skilled Grades 6 through 9 have more than doubled to 405.

Wage Rates

In reviewing South Africa wage rates, one must consider the special factors which have been generally operative in the South African labor market. First, wage rates for particular races have fluctuated with labor availability. As the South African economy rapidly expanded, the wage rates for the generally more highly skilled whites were driven upward, and additional Colored and Africans were absorbed into the labor force at the lower paying, less skilled jobs--and at wage rates lower than for whites.

Second, an ability factor exists; rather than a fixed wage for a specific job, a merit increase system allowed a wage differential based on the job performance of individuals doing the same work. Third, a seniority factor is operative; wages for a specific individual reflect length of time on the job.

All these factors worked toward wage rate differen-
tials among the races--forcing the national average for
whites far above that for other race groups.

In order to overcome these disparate forces, General
Motors South African has initiated a new wage program, very
similar to that in the United States. Under our new program, new employees receive the minimum starting wage shown
for each grade. After the first six months of employment,
an automatic increase is granted--with the remaining dis-
tance to the maximum wage representing recognition of ability and seniority factors. Promotion to a higher grade is
required to receive an increase above the stated maximum
for each grade. Considerable additional wage expense has
been incurred to reduce the differential between minimum
and maximum wage rates.

FIGURE 1

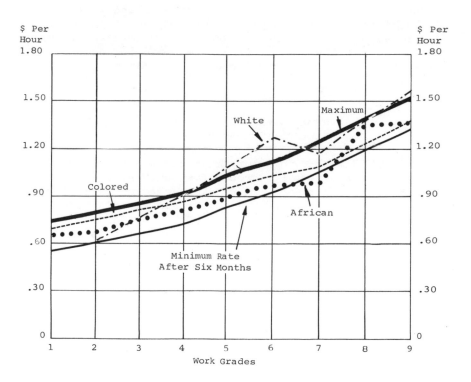

Figure 1 indicates the wage rates for multiracial work grades at GM South African. The average rates for white employees in Grades 5, 6, and 9 are above the maximum. Some employees of all race groups are receiving rates higher than the maximum due to merit increases and seniority under GM South African's previous wage program. Over the next 12 to 18 months, it is planned that the substantial portion of these individuals will fall within the new ranges as a result of training, which will permit advancement to a higher grade.

Although there is a gap between the average wage rates for races in comparable grades as shown here, considerable progress has been made in raising Colored and African wages and thereby reducing the wage differential between the races. In the past year and a half, Colored and African hourly employees have received an average wage rate increase of 23 percent, compared with 18 percent for whites.

In summary, GM South African's new wage system has reduced the wage differential by race in the work grades. It has increased the wages of Colored and Africans in order to establish a standardized wage structure through: (1) narrowing the wage differential paid for a specific job; and (2) initiation of a standard, minimal seniority system.

Average Male Wage Increases--
GM South African vs. Overall

Another measure of our progress is a comparison of the per capita income increase for South African males, as published recently by a private research group in South Africa, and the increase in wages paid to GMSA males in the last few years. As shown in Table 4, per capita income for Colored, African, and Asiatic males is now increasing at a greater rate than for whites. This trend is reflected at GM South African, where wage increases have exceeded the overall average.

As previously indicated, since March of 1971, average Colored and African wages at GMSA have increased 23 percent, compared with 18 percent for whites. This 23 percent increase also exceeded the average for all manufacturing in South Africa during the same period.

TABLE 4

Average Male Wage Increases--
GM South African vs. Overall
(in percent)

	12 Months Ending			Memo: Mar. 1971 to Oct. 1972
	April 1971	Nov. 1971	April 1972	
GM South African				
Colored and African	9	15	15	23
White	10	11	12	18
Overall Male Per Capita Income				
Colored, African, and Asiatic	8	8	12	18
White	11	7	5	7

Other Employment Steps

Several other employment steps have been taken by
GMSA to improve communication with its Colored and African workers and to assure its continued progress and
identity.

An African Works Committee was elected in the fall
of 1971 to represent African employees. This committee
has met regularly with management to discuss matters of
mutual interest. In this regard, three African shop stewards have been appointed to represent African employees
and have been given the same privileges and responsibilities as the stewards representing our Colored and white
employees.

As I indicated earlier, the first Colored foreman at
GM South African was recently appointed, and more are expected in the near future. Two Colored hourly employees
have also been assigned as Quality Control Inspectors in
the body shop. This is the first time that employees
other than whites have held these positions at GM South
African. All areas are continually under review for further appointments of this nature.

The abilities of our employees are regularly reviewed in order that they can be directed into training
programs commensurate with their potential.

Training

GM South African has an extensive range of training programs to upgrade its Colored and African employees and provide a basis for upward job mobility. Training for new hires and on-the-job training are provided for all employees. In addition, five specific training programs are in operation, with all costs paid by the company. Fifty-six Colored and African employees have satisfactorily completed literacy instruction in a Basic Training Program, and fourteen more are currently enrolled in this program.

Thirty-three Colored employees have successfully completed instruction on the first phase of a Technical Training Program, and thirty-nine employees are taking advantage of the program at the present time. Eight Colored repair shop assistants are participating in a Workshop Technician Training Program.

Since 1970, 257 Colored and African employees have participated in a Pre-Supervisory Training Program. Twenty-three who completed this training have already been appointed to supervisory positions. It was a graduate of this training program who recently became the first Colored foreman at GM South African. Further, since 1954 the GM South African Service Division has operated a fully equipped Mobile Training Unit which provides instruction to dealer service personnel. Since June of 1971, over 200 Colored, African, and Indian personnel have received training on dealer premises throughout South Africa in skills such as sheet metal repair, spray painting, and general mechanical maintenance. In the future, courses will be held in the African homelands, with the unit scheduled to visit Swaziland and Botswana.

Employee Plans

GM South African's efforts extend into many areas beyond the basic employment relationship. Employee plans apply to all employees, regardless of race. Benefits include group life insurance and medical, sickness and accident, and retirement plans. Improved group life insurance and retirement plans have recently been approved and will be put into effect early next year.

The medical plan also covers dependents of employees, as well as retirees and their dependents. In July of this year, the medical plan was expanded to provide coverage for dental care, routine physical examinations, and eye examinations. In addition, all employees receive a thorough prehire medical examination, annual chest X-rays, and emergency medical service. A doctor and four nurses, including one Colored and one African, administer these programs at our facilities.

GM South African benefit plans provide benefits at least equal to the average for all race groups in South Africa and, with regard to Colored and African employees, our benefits are well above those provided by most other companies in South Africa.

As to educational assistance, 29 Colored and African employees are furthering their formal education by participating in the Tuition Refund Plan. In 1972, 124 high school scholarships have been granted to children of African and Colored employees. Further, almost 500 children of our African employees are taking advantage of a bursary plan which covers the cost of prescribed books and school fees for children. Booklets on these plans, as well as booklets on our training and educational programs, have recently been distributed to our employees.

Outside Educational and Financial Assistance

GM South African continues to render financial assistance to organizations dedicated to furthering the progress of the Colored and African people of South Africa. Reflecting a thorough examination of GM South African's outside educational and financial assistance programs, contributions made to Colored and African organizations this year will represent 43 percent of our total support, compared with 5 percent in 1969. (In addition, 34 percent of total contributions in 1972 were made to organizations representing all races.)

Among the numerous organizations supported by General Motors are the Inanda Seminary for Girls, the South African Institute of Race Relations, the Association for the Educational and Cultural Advancement of the African People of South Africa, the Bureau of Adult Literacy, the United States-South Africa Leader Exchange Program, and The African-American Institute. In addition, GM South African has contributed through the National Study Loan and Bursary Fund to one Colored and three African universities.

Housing Assistance and Recreational Facilities

GM South African recognizes that the dwellings occupied by many of its Colored and African employees are a serious social problem. Accordingly, meetings have been held with municipal authorities to consider various proposals for housing assistance to our employees.

As a first step, on a priority basis, the company has arranged to lend a number of Colored employees the necessary down payment to buy their homes.

We have also reviewed other ways in which we might improve the social well-being of our Colored and African employees. Through the years, our employees in South Africa have manifested a great interest in athletics. In order to fulfill these needs, the construction of rugby, cricket, and soccer fields, a tennis court, a clubhouse, and other related facilities in the Colored residential area has recently been approved. After implementation of this project, comparable recreational facilities will be available to our Colored and white employees. In addition, a similar recreational plan for African employees is being considered.

SUMMARY

The South African situation admittedly involves complex issues on which reasonable men can differ. Our continuing approach is to improve the economic status of our employees and to build a climate within which desired changes can be implemented. On this basis, our continued operation in South Africa is consistent with the best interests of our stockholders and South African employees.

Although the South African economy has slowed over the past two years, indications point to an economic upturn in 1973. Similarly, the outlook for the automobile industry in South Africa is favorable. Total vehicle registrations are expected to increase to approximately 300,000 vehicles in 1973. GM South African expects to participate in this growth and to improve its overall market position. In the long term, South Africa represents a tremendous opportunity for the automobile and commercial vehicle business.

The South African economy offers considerable opportunities for sound economic growth. The African, Colored, and Asian sectors of the population should benefit as they become more closely integrated into industrial and commercial life, not only in the African homelands and border areas but throughout the country. Employment opportunities will improve, and wages and salaries will show a corresponding increase. The fact that white trade unions are allowing other race groups to occupy jobs of greater

skill and importance and the demand by the Trade Union
Council of South Africa for recognition of African trade
unions indicate these trends toward greater opportunities
for all races.

In conclusion, General Motors believes that the steps
taken during the last two years represent substantial
progress in upgrading our Colored and African employees.
Our total program for upgrading our work force is a broad
one. The areas on which we can be criticized are steadily
being reduced, and I hope in the not too distant future
you will be able to join with us in celebrating the attainment of our mutual objective, equal opportunities in
South Africa. We will continue to review all areas for
further progress. General Motors will remain in South
Africa and will continue to be in the forefront of progressive change.

<u>Donald McHenry</u>: General Motors has, to its credit, responded to the great concern about developments in South Africa. I should also say that having seen the situation at close hand, particularly over the last year, and considering the presentation by Mr. Estes, a significant amount of change has occurred.

In fact, I think that the presentation is an indication of what can be done once the decision is made to try to make advances in some of these areas. At the same time it gives us some indication as to the kinds of questions we should ask. One such question is whether management itself should be trusted to act alone in some of these areas. I mean no insult to General Motors when I say that.

Many of the changes that are demonstrated by Mr. Estes are changes which had not been made prior to the criticism and pressure which came from church groups and some other groups, as Mr. Estes pointed out in his statement. This alone indicates that there is a need and a role for the concerned outsider when it comes to influencing business.

One can see in the last year at General Motors, as well as in a number of other firms, the kind of changes that have been, frankly, long overdue. You do have new management there. You do have planning now, and not planning just on the local level, but planning which is also done back here in the United States. This is in sharp contrast to the situation which had previously existed. There was a colossal ignorance on the part of home offices about many of the things which were of great concern.

FUNDAMENTAL QUESTIONS REMAINING

There remain, however, some rather fundamental questions that are only partially exposed in Mr. Estes's presentation. There is no question that there are increases in wages and increases in fringe benefits. This is an improvement in the life of General Motors employees, insofar as General Motors to this point has control over it.

But there are South African Government limitations on action in some of these areas. Take, for example, some of those programs that Mr. Estes has mentioned in the area of housing. It is true that Colored* workers are assisted in their down payments on houses. There was even a statement that consideration is being given to assistance for Africans. However, in South Africa the position of the Colored and the African employee is so different that the amount of assistance General Motors, or any firm, can give in the area of African housing is extremely limited. Even with assistance, Africans still must live in a township and are not able to break out of the social and political pattern that exists there. No matter what an American firm does in the way of housing, this kind of problem, which is inherent in the South African social and political system, remains.

You can also see continuing limitation in the area of job advancement. Mr. Estes points out that General Motors follows a policy of equal opportunity, an affirmative policy where people performing like work get the same pay. He states that there is equal opportunity for advancement. In point of fact, this is only partially true. There remain both explicit and implicit limits as far as the level to which nonwhite employees can rise. There is explicit job reservation, which is suspended in the case of the automobile industry, but which is nevertheless on the books and remains the foundation for the basic South African labor system. It remains the lever which forces

---

*South Africa officially divides its population into racial and ethnic groups. The terms "Colored," "Bantu," and "Asian" refer to groups of mixed, African, and Asian ancestry, respectively. The term "nonwhite" is frequently used to refer to the three groups collectively. These terms are used below to facilitate the discussion and in no way imply acceptance or approval by the consultation participants of their use, especially in light of the distinct disapproval by the groups themselves.

General Motors and other firms constantly to negotiate
with white unions, and constantly places in jeopardy the
height to which the African employee can rise. Moreover,
the government has stated very clearly that no nonwhite
can supervise a white employee. This obviously means that
an employer must create a situation where he has an all
nonwhite section in order to have a nonwhite supervisor.
The number of areas where the nonwhite can rise to higher
positions is extremely limited. In practice, therefore,
it would seem to me that there really are not equal opportunities there for all. There are equal opportunities
within very clearly defined limits.

Another area one could point out where development is
needed is the area of education. One can establish scholarship programs, as General Motors has done. One can set
up bursary programs as they have done, and that is a considerable advancement over the situation which had previously existed. As far as the Africans are concerned, General Motors is involved, or potentially involved, in their
education from the very beginning through to the university
level.

This, too, is a considerable advancement; but the
problem emerges when one compares the situation at GM with
the general situation in South Africa. General Motors,
after all, is not in the business of education--it is in
the business of making cars, and its education program is
to assist its employees to this end. The educational system of South Africa is one which unfairly discriminates
against nonwhites. This inevitably limits the effectiveness of any kind of education program that General Motors
could establish on the inside.

Even though GM has a program of scholarship assistance for nonwhites, the truth is that less than one percent of the African population rises to the level where
they can use the high-school scholarship. Thus, the effectiveness of programs in this area depends not alone on
what the American company does, or the British company, or
even the South African company for that matter; it depends
upon the social and political situation that exists outside the plant, outside the corporate context.

After one has made significant advances within the
plant, one is still faced with the stark reality of the
structure of the South African society, where the social
and political structure of apartheid continues to exist.
One has in essence improved the life of one's own employees, but has not improved the life of others. Even the
improvement in the lives of the corporations' employees

is limited. Nothing has been done to eliminate or to affect the more than 200 laws that the South African Government has introduced since 1948 that severely restrict the
social and political life of the nonwhite employees. Moreover, no matter how one conducts business, no matter how
many benefits or improvements in working conditions are in-
stituted, one still is, in essence, helping the economy.

THE CENTRAL ISSUE: ECONOMIC
DEVELOPMENT AND CHANGE

The question one faces in considering the whole South
African situation is a philosophical one. What does economic development in the long term contribute to the destruction of the social and political system that is apartheid? I think we have tended to get simple answers to
that question. It is an article of faith with American
businessmen, and an article of faith with many in the United States, that somehow our continued presence and contributions to the economy are going to break down the
structure of apartheid in the long term. Mr. Estes implied this in his own statement.

However, this runs in the face of the only hard research that we have in this area, and it runs in the face
of recent developments. South Africa has recently en-
joyed a great economic boom. The boom was greatest in
South Africa in the 1960s. It was precisely at that time
that the more obnoxious laws of the system were introduced and the social and political grip that the whites
hold over the nonwhites in this system tightened.

Secondly, Herbert Adams, in Modernizing Racial Domi-
nation, is able to point out--the book considers a period
of 50 years--that far from modernization and industrialization having contributed to the breaking down of traditional patterns in South Africa, the system simply seems
to adapt to the new changes. Yesterday the whites held
the job of semiskilled and skilled employees (blue collar
jobs), and the Africans held the jobs of laborers, floor
sweepers, etc. Tomorrow--and we see this already--non-
whites will be moving up to semiskilled and in some cases
skilled jobs that the whites had previously held; but the
whites will have moved up to the front office.

The gap in both wages and social structure remains
the same. It is just a new kind of gap. Adams is not
alone in his view. Industrialization and Race, a book
published in the United Kingdom more than 50 years ago,

97

studies about five or six social systems, including the United States. The conclusion is inescapable: Unless there is some kind of definite government input during economic development, racial discrimination will continue to exist. Certainly if one looks at our practice here in the United States, it would appear that without the strong government action taken in the 1960s the patterns would be the same in the United States, and discrimination would continue.

I must stress that business executives are caught in a series of conflicts, and resolving them is very, very difficult. There is obviously a desire with all multinational corporations to move toward local management, and yet moving toward local management in the South African situation may further cement local social and political attitudes. Businesses wish to maintain maximum control over what they consider their business responsibilities, yet if businesses operate in the South African situation they find themselves giving up or having to share control with the government on internal management questions. Business is told what kinds of signs to have over the toilets, how many entrances the plant must have, how many doors the first-aid room must have, how much one may expand and where, and what kind of labor may be used in this expansion. All of these kinds of controls are obviously ones that business does not want to tolerate.

Clearly the desire is to abide by local custom, to be as much a part of the country where one is operating as possible. Yet to abide by social and political custom in South Africa is to be in dramatic conflict with those minimum standards that one has learned and has reason to use in his own country. These conflicts are not readily resolved, even by the kinds of imaginative programs that Mr. Estes has presented.

THE COMPLEXITY OF THE ISSUE

Timothy Smith: Two or three years ago, when looking at General Motors and at American business generally, we-- some church people, some people in the black community, "critics" of U.S. business in South Africa--found that business supported racism in South Africa in two ways. One, an obvious area, was the labor conditions in plants. I think we have seen in the General Motors presentation that there is considerable latitude when the home company sincerely desires to alleviate this problem. But we must

get beyond just the labor conditions in the plant--you
have to weigh more than what you are paying your workers.
You have to look at the role of the company and the whole
economic structure and the use of products, etc. Chrysler,
General Motors, and Ford should evaluate the role they
have played in the economy itself.

The South African Government has been very clever in
demanding that products be built with a certain percentage
of local content. This content is now approaching close
to 70 percent, I believe. Thus the auto industry has become a real catalyst in the whole economic boom in South
Africa. It has become a real catalyst in building local
industries and in encouraging local industries. We must
ask questions about whether this is not really an encour-
agement for building an economic strength for the white
minority in power in South Africa.

We have to ask questions such as: Will General
Motors in the future continue to give money, as it did in
1969, to the South African Foundation, a foundation that
fosters white supremacy attitudes overseas? What have
General Motors and other companies done in the United
States in terms of talking about what is happening in
South Africa? What is General Motors' strategic or mili-
tary significance in South Africa? What influence might
General Motors have in the United States Government in a
time of crisis in South Africa? What will South Africa--
and GMSA--do as the liberation struggle moves south from
Angola and Mozambique, as it continues to flare up in
Rhodesia, and possibly one day erupts in South Africa?
We are dealing with a system here. We are asking ques-
tions about the strengthening not simply of the labor system of the General Motors plant, but of white control in
South Africa itself.

We must criticize companies that are building myths
about South African change. Currently South Africa is
locked into white supremacy. But real change in South
Africa means that the majority must rule. As far as black
South Africa is concerned, change means changing the political system, not just allowing a few more people in
higher jobs or higher job levels. Real change means
changing the total system, allowing black people in South
Africa to have real social and economic power rather than
being a subservient race in a nation of white supremacy.

Charles Powers: It seems to me that in response to Don
McHenry, General Motors could have two basic answers.
One is that economic development will bring an end to the

racism in South Africa. The other is that racism is so
endemic to the South African situation that the company
that does in fact provide the types of programs that General Motors is trying to provide for its employees is doing more good than harm within a basically hopeless situation. If you support the economic development view, you
should at all points be pushing to demonstrate that economic development can bring an overall improvement. No
such evidence was given in the presentation.

On the other hand if you believe there is so much
racism there that there is no hope, then you should stop
giving arguments with respect to how things have gotten
better in the last two years. Which way does General Motors see this scenario, and why do you see it that way?

Mr. Estes: I don't know whether we will ever be able to
settle here in this discussion the argument that possibly
American companies are contributing to the economy in
South Africa. The question is, and our position is, that
if it is true on one side, it is far outweighed by the
benefit of setting examples and moving toward progressive
change on the other side. Maybe we have to wait five
years, and if we don't have a confrontation in the mean-
time, which might happen, we will see how this works out.

STATUS QUO OR REAL CHANGE?

Mr. Smith: There is fighting in Angola and Mozambique
that has been going on for ten years. There is political
action inside Rhodesia. One has to ask what the role is
of the American government and American business with regard to the war in all of southern Africa, in which Black
Africa obviously lines up on the side of the nationalists.

The white West seems lined up on the side of existing
governments in southern Africa. We cannot pretend that
this fact does not exist. I would hope that we have
learned the lesson from Vietnam that we must be very careful in analyzing how American involvement occurs.

I fear that we will think that we need to protect our
vested interests at certain times. Will General Motors be
forced, at some point, to share the analysis of the South
African Government that the nationalists moving south are
Communists and that they are trying to get rid of white
Christian civilization? I hope we never hear that speech.
But could that be something forced on corporations by the
threat to their vested interests at some time? For

example, there is the nationalist movement moving toward
the sea in Angola. Will Gulf Oil find ways to protect its
operations in Angola? Will the U.S. Government be involved in such protection? These are all questions that
we have to ask, because they bring us into the mix of
American corporate and government life that too often has
been set on the side of the status quo rather than on the
side of real change.

Mr. Estes: It could be that through evolutionary change
and economic benefits we are going to be able to move
slowly, and move up, and that what has taken place in
South Africa in the last two years is going to be the nu-
cleus of a change. The alternative as I see it, and I
hate to say this, might be bloody confrontation. We will
not have our corporation get mixed up in that if we can
help it. We want to avoid it.

I don't know whether some of the critics, and the
people there, are really promoting a confrontation. Is
that the idea, to get this thing fixed quickly? It seems
to me that it is better to try to do it over a period of
time.

I see improvement. There has been a movement toward
the freedom of the Coloreds and the Africans in the last
two or three years. Whether we can continue or whether
we are going to have trouble, I don't know.

QUESTIONS OF FOREIGN POLICY

Dr. Powers: The key question always comes down to whether
or not the United States foreign policy is importantly determined, or would in the case of rapid change be determined, by the U.S. corporate presence. Is there in the
foreseeable future any possibility that U.S. corporations,
either singly or together, may reach an understanding with
the U.S. Government that it has no obligation to protect
U.S. corporate investment should it see progressive new
possibilities for foreign policy that are contrary to private economic interests?

Mr. Estes: As far as our dealing with the State Department goes, we are thinking exactly the same. South Africa
has to move--to try to change the attitude there and implement gradual movement toward the freedom of these
people. We both agree on this method, and I believe that
it is pretty much in agreement with our current policy as
I have expressed it here.

If your question is what is going to happen, what the government's attitude is going to be in the case of a revolution or movement by militants to make some other than gradual change, we will have no part in that. If there is a confrontation of that kind, we are certainly not going to have any part of it.

There is a problem with regard to protection. There are General Motors interests, of course, in South Africa, but they are relatively minor--it is a very small part of our business.

RISING EXPECTATIONS

Jon Gunnemann: There is a certain peculiar irony about what General Motors is doing. The process of promoting people, or educating people, is going to raise expectations. In doing this, you are going to contribute to a situation where the system, whatever it is and whoever is responsible for it, cannot produce what the heightened expectations require. Therefore I think that one of the things you have to face is the possibility that you are going to be causing some kind of a confrontation.

Mr. Estes: Isn't that a better problem to face than the other?

Prof. Gunnemann: It is a much better problem, but what I am trying to say involves two things. First, I would suggest that simple economic development, even if it goes across the board, does not in itself mean that you have gradual social and political change. You can create radical change with the best of intentions. Secondly, the response companies make when they begin to see that things might start getting out of control is critical. This is not a criticism so much as a suggestion that there is a lot more in the future.

Mr. Estes: We will discuss that next year.

11

CHALLENGES TO
CORPORATE RESPONSIVENESS

THE NEED FOR PRODDING FROM WITHOUT

Robert Potter: Why was it necessary for General Motors and other groups of motor corporations to be dragged kicking and fuming into the South African issue raised by church groups regarding the plight of black employees? Do you personally continue to have what appears to outsiders to be a strongly hostile response when a group puts up a resolution, asking you formally to disclose what you are doing in South Africa? You hire eminent counsel over here to fight us, and we go down to the SEC just to find out what you are doing. Is this going to continue ad infinitum, year after year?

Why this concept? What are you scared of? What are you going to gain? Why didn't you throw your cards on the table and discuss it as you are doing today?

E. M. Estes: Are you saying, why didn't we give this pitch a year and a half ago? If some stockholders had asked for some disclosure in South Africa, then we would have. The first church-supported resolution asked us to get out of South Africa.

I think, as I said a while ago, that there is no question that our minds are changing, that we are becoming more progressive, and I hope that we are becoming more responsive to the needs of people, whether they are our stockholders, customers, or whatever. When you asked us for disclosure, we made a disclosure on this subject last February, and it took us only another six months to give you the whole picture. We have given you everything you have asked for here except one thing, and that is our

103

profit. We have problems, sure we have, and we have to clean them up. Maybe I am expressing a different attitude than we had three years ago, and if I am I was chief engineer or something like that at that time, worrying about whether the car would run. Maybe we have changed, and if we have, give us credit for it.

Mr. Potter: I think that, looking ahead, business's credibility would be very much improved if you were more open, and not afraid to say, as you have said here today, "From 1947 to 1967 we stank, we finally recognized it, and we are trying to improve the situation."

J. Howard Craven: The heart of the issue as I see it is this: We all agree that there is an odious regime someplace that none of us likes. Some people take the position that you have to fight it, and other people take the position that you have to change it from within. I take the position that if you are concerned about the well-being of the people in an area where you dislike the regime you still continue to work and try to improve the position of those people in the country.

Other people take the position that you have to destroy the economy, you have to make the conditions so intolerable that the economy cannot last despite the fact that the people you are trying to help are the people who are going to suffer from the destruction of the economy.

I don't like the social regime in South Africa, but I think it is true that if you try to remove American investments and succeed in doing so you would not benefit black people in South Africa. I think that it is false to assume that an attempt to keep investment out of a country that you don't like would in any way be an effective means of stopping the social deterioration.

CONSIDERING LONG-TERM CORPORATION IMPACT

Kirk O. Hanson: Let me express a discomfort about the whole approach toward engagement that General Motors is taking. There seems to be an assumption that the engagement-disengagement question is primarily a moral issue, each side attempting to establish the purity of its moral purpose and belief about the justice or injustice of the conditions in South Africa. Instead I believe we have to think very much in terms of a strategy we are trying to construct that will have some impact on

improving conditions in South Africa. Pressed by the
kinds of concerns that have been directed toward General
Motors and other corporations, General Motors has re-
sponded by citing the areas in which they make and have
made improvements.

However the proper response would be the forming of
a strategy that will have the greatest long-run impact.
I think that it is a copout to say that these are the
areas where we can make improvements and we will continue
on that course until we run "up against a wall." Instead
we should be dealing with the question of what kind of
overall strategy is going to make improvement. I don't
see, considering the overall issue, what the long-run impact of your changes will be.

Mr. Estes: If you have some suggestions as to long-range
progress--what we should do at General Motors--I'll mark
them down, and we will put them into effect. I can assure
you that if there is an impression here that we are trying
to fix the situation only long enough to get by this conference, for instance, that would be ridiculous. Our
plans are all long-range, and the long-range plan is to
get the proper proportion of Africans and Colored in our
organization. There is nothing we would like better than
20 years from now to have an African running our subsidiary there. If anybody has a suggestion on the long-range
policy, or a long-range program other than what we have
outlined here, we certainly would be responsive to it.

Mr. Hanson: The overall social and political structure
outside the work environment is most critical. The question is, does General Motors feel that it has any role,
any responsibility, in terms of the improvement of the
overall lot of the Colored and the African? If indeed
they do, then the concern for just the work environment
is not enough. The questions that have been asked of you
as to what kinds of cooperation are you willing to undertake in order to try to make more extensive changes within
the country are appropriate questions.

Donald McHenry: I look at the engagement-disengagement as
a tactic. I think that if the church groups and others
had not put a great deal of pressure on the "get-out" side
we would not have had any of this dramatic movement that
we have had during the last couple of years on the "improvement" side. But, as I have said, I am most interested in any plans that business has made for actively
affecting the broader social and political situation.

It would be gratifying, for example, to see a company helping to organize African workers, helping them to organize in an effective manner, and then negotiating with them, even though such activity does not have the sanction of law.

This would be an effort to show the government and the people that this kind of thing is possible, that it is not disastrous. It seems to me that this kind of device, right now at variance with the general social and political system, would have a positive effect. One is playing with fire in South Africa by doing these kinds of things, but it seems to me that this will have to be done if one is going to attack the social and political problems that remain after you increase wages and job opportunities.

Mr. Estes: Our intention is to do what you said, but maybe we are not accomplishing it.

CAN CORPORATIONS BE "ACTIVISTS"?

Philip Moore: I find the whole issue of American business involvement in South Africa perplexing for the activist. I agree with Mr. McHenry that the debate between disengagement and engagement sort of misses the point. Certainly going after disengagement may suggest a good strategy, but for now General Motors must consider what they should do short of disengagement. Given what was said earlier about General Motors having done little until two years ago, the proposal to withdraw from South Africa must have done something to force General Motors to act. What should the activists do in order to keep General Motors acting? It seems clear that it is only from the prompting of outside organizations that change occurs.

Do you think that the changes that you are beginning to make in South Africa are going to continue as these activist pressures diminish? Will General Motors in South Africa take it on its own and go into some areas through more activist channels?

Mr. Estes: Our feeling at the moment is to continue to do everything we can do to get people trained, get blacks where they belong, and move them up fast enough so that we are progressing as fast as we can right now, without confrontation. Let us take up all that slack before we start worrying about whether we have an open confrontation with the government with regard to the laws. This is our present strategy, right or wrong.

Horace Gale: Mr. Estes, with regard to existing profit
goals assigned to South Africa, what is the possibility of
a South African manager making expenditures for social
change, for instance, for training programs? Also, as
General Motors continues to work for changes in South Africa, do you see any benefits in joining with other foreign employers to press the government for improvement of
social and political conditions for Coloreds and Africans?

Mr. Estes: Naturally General Motors is in the business of
making a profit, so GMSA is a profit center in and of itself. As far as budgetary limitations on the number of
people who can join the training program, there is no
limit. We have no restriction on that.

Taking advantage of our training program, and so on,
is just a matter of how many people we can get interested.
We have been very displeased with the participation in
these programs. I think there were two reasons for it.
One was that we did not do a proper job of advertising--
informing our people about the program. Consequently, in
the last year, we have put out booklets to every employee
to let them know what is available to them.

Second, there was the disbelief, on the part of the
Africans particularly, that they were ever going to be
able to be a foreman, or be able to take advantage of
these situations. I think we have now moved, and we have
proven that these people do have an opportunity, that we
will advance them--whether it be an auto mechanic training
program, making a Colored person a foreman, or whatever it
is. I think that we are going to see some increased participation. There is no budget limitation on that at all.

The real problem, then, is that some of our competitors are still paying 20¢ an hour for labor. Our minimum
wage is currently somewhere around 56¢ or 53¢ an hour at
the start, and after six months advances to 63¢. We have
a real problem competitively. If we are going to stay in
business and do our best, we have to make a profit there.
We must have a good viable organization, or we are not
going to accomplish the kind of thing that we are talking
about.

I think that our problem right now is taking up the
slack that is available to us. We have to be able to set
up our training programs and be able to move people into
positions. This we can do right now. Currently we have
only two areas from a skilled trade point of view that
are problems, and we expect to get them fixed very soon.
We can put apprentices in programs, but we cannot get the

white union to agree to train the people. Consequently, we have to break this barrier. We have broken it as far as auto mechanics are concerned, and have people in that program.

Mr. Gale: Do you still have a problem there?

Mr. Estes: We used to have a problem.

Mr. McHenry: You still have a problem in the auto mechanics area, and this gets back again to the broader problem. By law there is nothing which says that a nonwhite cannot go under the apprentice program; but in fact in 1971 there were no Africans in approved apprentice programs in South Africa outside the so-called "homelands." In fact, in 1972 there were no African apprentices outside the "homelands." The Colored and Asian participation in that program was a little better. The point is that the social structure is such that Africans particularly are kept out of apprentice programs.

Mr. Estes: We have a policy of equal employment, but trying to implement it down there is difficult. We have a policy, and we try. We can have all the policy we want in the United States, but we have to get local white foremen in South Africa to implement these programs. It is not easy because of the social and political structure that we have been talking about. In the area of moving people up in the organization, it is a long process trying to train these people, to get them prepared for the jobs, and to get them interested enough to join our training programs, because I don't believe they think that they will be advanced. We have to prove that they will be.

INDEX

Adams, Herbert: on indus-
trialization in South
Africa, 97
American Can Company, 38
American Metal Climax Cor-
poration: operations in
Puerto Rico, 34–35
AMEX (see American Metal
Climax Corporation)
Angola: and Gulf Oil Cor-
poration, 19; and liber-
ation struggle, 99–101

Bauer, Raymond: on cor-
porate social audit,
xvi, 26–30, 34; on
managerial initiative,
18
Botswana: and GM Mobile
Training Unit, 90
Brandeis, Louis: on cor-
porate managers, xv

Chase, Howard: on struc-
turing social concerns
into decision-making,
70–71
Connole, Anthony W.: on
managerial responsibil-
ity, 15–16; on mana-
gerial professionalism,
16; on multinational
corporate responsibil-
ity, 16; on structuring
social concerns into
decision-making, 74–75
corporate accountability:
as prerequisite to cor-
porate responsibility,
xviii–xix (see also
social audit)

Council on Economic Priorities: and corporate social
audit, 27
Council on Religion and International Affairs: and Conference on Corporate and
Investor Responsibility, xiv
Craven, J. Howard: on General
Motors South African, 104
CRIA (see Council on Religion
and International Affairs)

Dreyfus Twentieth Century
Fund: and corporate social
audit, 42

EEO (see Equal Employment Opportunity)
Eldredge, Lincoln: on corporate advisory panel, 63–
64; on GM's Public Policy
Committee, 63–64
Episcopal Church: and GM
proxy controversy, xiv; and
South Africa, 43
Equal Employment Opportunity,
37, 38
Estes, E. M., xiv; on GM's
Public Policy Committee, 48,
65–66, 68–69; on General
Motors South African, 78,
100, 101–102, 103–104, 105–
108

Farber, Stephen B.: on managerial options for decision-
making, 19; on GM's Public
Policy Committee and public
disclosure, 66–67
Fenn, Dan H., Jr., xvi; on
corporate social audit,
26–27

RICHARD A. JACKSON is a graduate student at the
Divinity School, Yale University. Mr. Jackson, who has
studied and traveled in Ethiopia, India, Taiwan, and
Japan, holds a B.A. from St. Olaf College (1972), where
he majored in History and Asian Studies.

THE BANKS OF CANADA IN THE COMMONWEALTH CARIBBEAN:
Economic Nationalism and Multinational Enterprises
of a Medium Power
Daniel J. Baum

INTERNATIONAL CONTROL OF FOREIGN INVESTMENT:
The Dusseldorf Conference on Multinational
Corporations
edited by Don Wallace, Jr.
assisted by Helga Ruof-Koch

THE MULTINATIONAL CORPORATION AS A FORCE IN
LATIN AMERICAN POLITICS: A Case Study of the
International Petroleum Company in Peru
Adalberto J. Pinelo

MULTINATIONAL CORPORATIONS IN WORLD DEVELOPMENT
United Nations Department of
Economic and Social Affairs

THE MULTINATIONAL ENTERPRISE AND THE THIRD WORLD:
The Nationalization of Alcan-Dembe
I. A. Litvak and C. J. Maule

THE POLITICAL RISKS FOR MULTINATIONAL ENTERPRISE
IN DEVELOPING COUNTRIES: With a Case Study of Peru
Dolph Warren Zink

STRATEGIC AND LONG-RANGE PLANNING FOR THE
MULTINATIONAL CORPORATION
John Snow Schwendiman